EMOTIONAL REGULATION

FOR KIDS

GUIDING YOUNG MINDS

Resilience, ADHD, Therapy Techniques and Modern Digital Tools

Hopeful Hearts Publishing

CONTENTS

INTRODUCTION

DO YOU RECALL MAKING the mistake of walking through the children's toys aisle? Perhaps you thought it would be a nice distraction or cute to show your kid the colorful new figurines or giant stuffed toys, but for a minute, you completely forgot about the last time your little one became enamored with an object they just had to have. Unfortunately, this trip goes a bit awry as your kid sees the most amazing giant plush elephant that rivals their minute size. They *need* to have this plushy, but it's not on the agenda for today, and it's definitely not in this week's budget. Distraught and in emotional agony, your little one drops to the floor and unravels in a bundle of sobs and shrieks, holding on to the plushy for dear life. We've all been through these public meltdowns and epic tantrums. According to studies, about 50% of children have weekly tantrums (Salameh et al., 2021). So, what do we do to teach our little ones that rolling on the floor and shrieking is not the best course of action? Well, we just have to show them an alternative way to express themselves.

The Rollercoaster of Emotional Development

Recurring tantrums are only one aspect of parenting. Most people do not even know about the emotional reactions that happen at home. Before little ones understand their emotions, all they do is express themselves non-verbally. As they are developing, they express themselves through many different emotions. The laughter, smiles, and content looks are easy to understand, but when it comes to sadness, frustration, anger, or fear, we can become overwhelmed, stressed, and clueless about how to help our little ones through their ordeal. You have likely tried many different methods to calm your child down, such as comforting hugs, talking them down, giving them a treat, sitting them in front of their favorite show, or putting them in time-out. But it's just not working as it should! When your techniques aren't working, this doesn't mean you are an inadequate parent—it could mean that you're struggling with your child's emotional well-being.

As parents, we place a hefty burden on ourselves to be perfect, and when it doesn't all go to plan, even our emotions and behavioral expressions glitch. Frankly, no parent can be fully prepared for the journey of parenthood. Understanding our own emotions is important, and expressing ourselves is one of the key factors in practicing emotional regulation in our homes. So what's all the fuss about emotional regulation? Kids need to understand the way they feel, acknowledge why they feel the way they do, and express themselves in ways that do not cause self-harm or stunted growth so that they can flourish in a complex and wonderful society. Emotional well-being guides your little one in healthy behavior that ensures they enjoy themselves, are not bowled over by fear, and are excited by new challenges. An emotional regulation guide is what you need to support and encourage your child's social-emotional development and be the best parent you can be!

This book is filled with guidelines, tips, tools, and activities that will benefit not only your kids but you and your family as well. In this guide you are provided with:

- **Tailored strategies** to help your child through their different ages and developmental stages. As they move through different stages they experience emotions on new levels. Whether it's tantrums or a moody preteen phase, customized practical advice for your child's development helps you be their voice of reason.

- **A holistic approach** to emotional well-being that goes beyond controlling or managing your child's emotions, but aims to build a strong emotional foundation. Discover tips and activities designed to boost your child's self-esteem and emotional intelligence that promote harmonious family life in the long run.

- **Easily incorporate activities** that educate your child on emotional learning while keeping their curious minds engaged and having fun with them. Experience interactive outdoor activities that help express big emotions and center themselves and encourage emotional expression through arts and crafts to improve their self-understanding and build confidence.

- **A special focus on ADHD** for parents who deal with added challenges in emotion-based behavior. This book provides valuable insights, coping strategies, and techniques to improve your child's emotional competence, learn to understand themselves, and boost their self-love.

- **Advanced methodologies** in two different types of behavioral therapy that improve your child's cognitive, emotional, and social well-being. Emotional and behavioral challenges create a complex developmental journey but this book brings understanding and presents effective methods in a straightforward parent-friendly manner.

This book provides you with an important understanding of your child's experiences, what they are exposed to as they move through different stages in their life, and what it all looks like from their perspective. Understanding how your kid perceives the world and emotionally responds to it is important to incorporating healthy thoughts, behaviors, and a positive mindset. The world is full of challenges, obstacles, and undiscovered wonders. Improving your kid's self-regulation and understanding of themselves and the world—ensuring they blossom in whichever environment they find themselves in and face challenges head-on with confidence—is achieved through raising an emotionally resilient child. In this book, you will gain an understanding on the depth of emotional regulation and how to build it in children as young as the age of three; how to emotionally prepare them for preschool and guide them through hormone-induced emotions in the tween phase; understand the link between emotions, thought patterns, and the brain, and learn emotional learning activities; protect your kid from the dangers of social media; and fully understand the great role parents play in their kids healthy and happy development. If you want your kid to prosper in all their endeavors, this is the book for you!

Ready for Take-Off

Discover and implement these tools, tips, and techniques to develop emotional well-being in your home. Whether this is your first kid or your fifth, these techniques change your home for the better. Each child is different but these guidelines can be fit for all. These techniques are applicable to different age groups, learning styles, cognitive abilities, and temperaments to help you teach your kid self-awareness, boost their self-esteem and self-confidence, let them learn through experiences, teach them self-independence and responsibilities to develop their self-worth, build positive cognitive and emotional responses, and watch them bloom into well-rounded, happy, and resilient children. Raising children does not come with a manual, so use this book as your guide in the journey of parenthood.

CHAPTER 1

The A to Z of Emotional Regulation

—

S LOWLY INHALE A DEEP BREATH through your nostrils. Hold it in for ten seconds. Exhale gently through your mouth. Repeat this exercise about five times. Can you feel the difference? Deep breathing exercises help to center our minds during overwhelming periods. This practice releases physical tension, provides us with a momentary reprieve from troublesome thoughts, and brings our emotional responses into perspective. Breathing exercises are a basic form of emotional regulation. When we are emotionally triggered or anxious, our stress responses are alerted. One of the ways the body responds to this is by increasing your heart rate and breath rate. The way we counteract hyperventilation and a fight-or-flight response is to control and decrease our breathing rate, which is done through breathing exercises. Breath control reduces blood pressure and cortisol production, improves immune system functions, boosts energy levels, and fosters a sense of calm and overall well-being. Breathing exercises bring us back to reality and help us refocus on what's important. It helps us regain control of our thoughts and emotions and shapes our behavior.

What Is Emotional Regulation?

Do you recall a day when it all seemed like too much? Maybe you've had a busy week, and there is a list of things you still need to do. Instead of getting a day to simply exhale, you need to head to the store and stock up on groceries. And, of course, the little bugger decides that now is the time to undress, refuses to put on his or her shoes, and throws their body to the ground just as it's time to leave! This is probably the last thing you need today, and emotions are high. This is not the first tantrum or outburst of the day. One too many buttons have been pushed, patience has worn thin, and because time is of the essence, the enforcer parent comes out. So, now we're raising our voices, forcibly dressing the little one, throwing him or her over the shoulder, and strapping them into the car seat where they will hopefully stop wriggling. All the while, your little one has discovered a new pitch to their voice. Could there have been a different way to remedy the situation? What is the reason your little one has been so explosively expressive today? Perhaps they feel lonely today and simply want a little time with you. Are they picking up on your emotional turmoil and distress? Emotions can be contagious, especially if they are negative.

The art of emotional regulation simply lies in regulating your emotional responses. This self-development tool fosters greater emotional intelligence that guides and enhances interactions throughout life. Emotional regulation means working through your thoughts and emotions before responding. You are taking into account more than the emotions, thoughts, and actions that are flooding your mind during an interaction. Instead, you are acknowledging the context and climate of the interaction, who it is that you are communicating with, and their understanding of the topic at hand. You are taking into consideration the individual's feelings, how your tone will come across, and what the impact of the way you respond will be. The emotional regulation process may be a mental process that occurs during communication or after when you relate the interaction to friends or family and create a self-understanding of how it all progressed or how you could have responded better. Emotional regulation practices may also include meditation, journaling, introspection, therapy, self-care, and physical exercise to release frustrations.

We experience emotions every day and they can vary throughout the hours. Emotional regulation is important to both our internal and external exchanges. Effective regulation ensures that conflict is dealt with in a healthy manner and improves your overall well-being and relationships. Emotional regulation allows you to express yourself in a manner that mediates negative emotions and actions and should not be confused with emotional control. When we have a strong hold on our emotions, we are hoarding frustrations and bitterness that are often expressed as volatile interactions. Like in the example above, emotional control and volatile expressions often lead to self-injury, i.e., self-destructive feelings or expressions of guilt, shame, etc. Emotional regulation allows us to better control our emotional state (Klynn, 2021).

How Kids Express Their Emotions

Emotions can be short-lived but can be intense and create lingering effects. They are comprised of your subjective experience, a physiological response, and a behavioral or expressive response (Cherry, 2021). How we experience events and respond to them may be based on our temperament, understanding of the world, mindfulness, self-awareness, and emotional intelligence. The way we experience and respond to interactions differs from one person to the next and is subjective to the way we perceive ourselves, our capabilities, and different environments. Your physiological responses to these experiences can be hyperventilating during a confrontation or experiencing fear-induced heart palpitations. Physiological responses based on subjective experiences result in a specific form of behavioral or expressive responses. In response to work conflict (i.e., subjective experience), your physiological response may increase your breath rate due to feeling cornered, and your behavioral expression may be to verbally defend yourself. Emotional intelligence governs our physical expressions and body language. Developing emotional intelligence is gained through self-awareness, self-understanding, and emotional regulation. Early emotional regulation greatly defines how well an individual is able to communicate and thrive in social interactions.

As kids develop, they express themselves in many different ways. From screeching when testing out their vocal cords to throwing a sippy cup when unhappy, your little one is learning to express themselves as they become more self-aware and aware of their environment and their capabilities. The first three years of a little one's life are vital to their emotional development and expression, as well as their subsequent cognitive and social skills. When they are not yet able to verbally express themselves, babies are able to express themselves by drawing near to some individuals and withdrawing from others, smiling and giggling, or crying. During the first year of a baby's life, they may express primary emotions such as sadness, anger, curiosity, or joy. Primary emotions are our universal emotional experiences. In the second year, your baby will start to display secondary emotions such as guilt, frustration, or embarrassment. Secondary emotions are usually in response to the primary emotions expressed. For example, if your little one is angry about something, they will communicate this by displaying frustration through emotional and behavioral expressions. In the first two years of a kid's life, there is great development and opportunity for emotional maturity. As they become more self-aware and cognizant of their environment, they form routines and build attachments to these routines and their primary circle. Changes that they experience in these areas often result in emotional expressions as they come to terms with their norms being altered. Think of when you introduce formula or solid foods, try different veggies, or have to find alternative care when it's time to go back to work. These can all result in expressions of joy, interest, unhappiness, or anxiety.

When your little one matures into toddlerhood, they become even more self-aware of how they react and how you react to their expressions, and they learn how to soothe themselves, i.e., sucking their thumbs or hugging themselves when feeling sad or anxious. As they mature, they gain empathy, learn to observe emotions in others, and even provide comfort. How your kid's emotional competence improves is largely based on their natural temperament, who they interact with, and the type of emotional responses they observe from a parent, guardian, or caregiver. Emotional competency is comprised of how they express their emotions, what they know about how they feel or why they are expressing themselves as such, and how they regulate their emotions. Emotional regulation in kids is defined by how well they react to stimuli and changes and adapt their behavior.

Emotional Regulation in Early Childhood

Emotional regulation in kids begins with your emotional and behavioral responses as a parent, guardian, or caregiver during infancy. How you soothe, comfort, and nurture the little one teaches them what techniques help them feel better. They integrate these responses and feelings when developing self-soothing techniques and self-regulation. At this early age, how kids express themselves is pure and visceral. There is not much thought to it, they simply feel and need to let it all out. Let's analyze the universal expression of the explosive temper tantrum during the second year of development. This usually occurs as a result of feelings of intense frustration and not being able to express themselves in any other manner. As your little one develops their vocabulary and emotional understanding, they will be able to better communicate their frustrations, and temper tantrums will decrease. Healthy and positive expressions from a parent, guardian, or caregiver create a safe environment for the little one to express themselves; subsequently, they begin understanding what these emotions mean and how to identify their feelings. This self-awareness and self-understanding guide them to emotional regulation.

At every new age or development period, your little one is learning more about themselves, the emotions they experience, how this makes them feel, and how it makes them want to act. Around the age of three, a greater understanding of emotions develop, but there is still little impulse control. They are very in tune with their emotions and sensitive to their environment and the primary feelings they evoke. Such as a sudden burst of tears when it's raining and they cannot wear their favorite summer outfit or harboring their sibling's toy due to jealousy. Soon, emotional and behavioral expressions may escalate to biting or scratching each other. This is all absolutely normal and part of the little one's emotional and social development and growth as they learn what expressions are appropriate or not. Through these experiences, correcting their behavior, and having teaching moments, kids begin to understand their emotions and learn emotional regulation in different contexts. In the period of ages four to five, your little one begins to express themselves better. They are now able to label their emotions and verbally express the roots of the emotional distress or behavioral expression. At the preschool stage and as a result of socializing with other little ones of a similar age group, kids become more aware of their physical differences and even start questioning where they come from (Brennan, 2022). Cue the birds and the bees talk. As your little one develops, so do their imagination and interest in the world around them. An active imagination aids emotional and cognitive development through increasing curiosity and developing social behavior, i.e., imaginary friends or tea parties with stuffed animals. In this context, your little one can apply or act out emotional expressions and nurture their audience in the way you teach them.

Little ones modulate their behavior after the emotional expressions and behaviors they observe. How you self-regulate and behave toward them shapes their perceptions of emotions and reactions. Parental reactive behavior can lead to reactive or misbehavior in the little one. Kids are super observant and notice when we struggle with our behavior and temper. The younger your child is when observing your behavior, the more they will imitate and adopt your expressions. Parental modeling helps to teach self-regulation and emotional intelligence. Adopting warm and positive emotional responses, teaching techniques, and parenting styles helps develop greater self-regulation. Additionally, creating a positive emotional climate in your household fosters healthy emotional behavior. Emotional regulation continues to develop your kids' emotional well-being and behavioral responses well into adulthood. A healthy and positive emotional regulation from you goes a long way in protecting and fostering emotional, mental, and social resilience in your child.

Self-regulation and emotional regulation prepare your child for all the complex interactions and experiences that occur in the world. It teaches discipline, patience, empathy, mindfulness, self-awareness, and social awareness. As they mature, emotional regulation and intelligence teach them how to behave in different social contexts and control emotional impulses. The foundation for primary emotional regulation is created during early childhood and is built upon as they enter the education system, where they acquire additional emotional and cognitive skills through the various people they socialize with. Emotional regulation from early childhood into the preteen stage encourages feeling and understanding your emotions, working through emotions, introspection periods, healthy expressions, calming techniques for different ages, conflict management skills, learning problem-solving techniques, boosting your kids' self-esteem, encouraging self-awareness, and praising them when they display healthy emotional regulation.

How Emotional Regulation Benefits Us All

Emotional regulation skills during childhood enable your little one to become emotionally and mentally resilient. It lays a foundation of self-awareness and self-confidence essential to social skills and learning during their schooling years. The first few years of their life are a crucial period for developing and refining functions such as attention, inhibition, active memory, verbalizing their thoughts, and improving literacy skills needed for success in academia (Graziano et al., 2007). From birth to the age of five, your child is within the critical window of acquiring new information and development skills through learning and teaching. Emotional and self-regulation strengthen the foundation of learning and literacy skills needed throughout the schooling years. The ability to learn and succeed in school improves your child's chances of succeeding in life. Improved emotion regulation skills facilitate their ability to independently attend to and learn new information (Graziano et al., 2007). As we mature, we build on this foundation and acquire new knowledge, skills, and life tools needed to flourish in adulthood.

Emotional regulation is influenced by the home environment, social environments, cultural backgrounds, and acquired behaviors. Almost full brain development occurs by the age of three and is a function of the interaction between biology and experience. As a result, your child's social and emotional experiences play a critical role in the growth of the brain's architecture (Housman, 2017). Improving emotional skills, regulation, and competence ensures healthy behavior and understanding during this critical period of development. Developing emotional competence and self-regulation leads to long-term academic, personal, and social success (Housman, 2017). Self- and emotional regulation develops and maintains mental health and overall well-being. Emotional regulation helps us function in many different areas and in new environments as we age. It develops normative social, cognitive, and language skills and allows us to cope with daily tasks and environmental changes (Graziano et al., 2007). Emotional regulation will help your little one grow into someone who can take on the world and not be mowed over by it.

Emotional dysregulation, emotional incompetency, or consistent impulse control can make it a lot harder for your little one to thrive in social conditions, at school, or adapt to changes. Eventually, this can lead to stunted emotional and cognitive development due to limited experience, learning, and life skill development, as well as poor attention span or information retention, and planning and problem-solving skills. Emotional regulation directly affects cognitive processes and academic success. Self-regulation, emotional development, and behavioral control can ensure early academic success (Graziano et al., 2007). What and how we learn during childhood schooling prepares the foundation for lifelong learning and skill development essential to further education, relationships, and careers. Kids who understand their feelings and emotions go on to form stronger friendships with others as they can calm themselves down when triggered, flourish at school, handle or better express their moods, and release negative thoughts or emotions. Emotional regulation and health are important for the development of all ages.

Emotional Regulation and Becoming a Parent

Learning to regulate ourselves in different contexts or events occurs through experience. As a parent, guardian, or caretaker, have you noticed that you may have had to adjust the way you speak or act because there is a little one watching everything you do? When you become the one who has to take care of a baby, there are a lot of changes that occur to your thought processes, perceptions, and hormones that influence your behavior. During pregnancy and infancy, your brain secretes happy hormones that keep you alert to everything your little one is doing and will have you staring in awe. This sensitizes new parents to infant emotion cues and enhances the response to infant stimuli among both parents and non-parents (Rutherford,

2015). As infants develop, there are a lot more expressions and behaviors that are experienced. As they grow and learn new things about their voice and emotions, so do we as adults, who are the primary caretakers. You may find that you are tried and tested in different emotional areas as your child expresses themselves. As a parent, it is a common challenge to maintain and regulate our emotions when faced with a distressed and dysregulated child, while at the same time helping them to regulate themselves (Rutherford, 2015).

How we act or react in response to emotional conflict affects the emotional understanding, response, and expression of our kids. They first learn through observation. Many times, dysfunctional or volatile expression is rooted in parental emotional expression or behavior or the home environment in which they are raised. If we display high levels of anger toward our kids in frustrating situations, they are less likely to observe and learn effective emotional regulation responses (Morris et al., 2007). A negative home environment, including poor emotional expression from a parent or guardian, siblings who are volatile, or living in a dysfunctional, unpredictable neighborhood will affect how your kid regulates his or her emotions and learns to express themselves. As a result, they are at risk of becoming highly emotionally reactive due to frequent, unexpected emotional displays or emotional manipulations (Morris et al., 2007). As a parent, there is a great weight on our shoulders to guide our little ones to exhibit healthy behavior and emotional expression, which will develop their mental and emotional health. Emotional teaching and a healthy parenting style through self-regulation help guide our kids to develop happier and healthier habits.

Emotional Regulation: A Two-Way Street

Practicing and teaching emotional regulation is a learning moment for both the child and the parent or caretaker. Your little one is discovering and labeling new emotions and feelings as they are exposed to different events or environments. How they learn to navigate their emotions is up to you. How you react to your own and your little one's emotional turbulence guides their behavior when faced with the same emotion or behavioral expression. Their emotional expressions and behavior force you to adjust or express yourself differently or more gently. This is a learning curve for both of you as emotional regulation in both the child and primary caretaker is further developed or refined. Parents who recognize their emotions and express themselves well are better able to guide their little ones on emotional regulation.

To improve our child's emotional and self-regulation skills, we have to prioritize our own emotional and mental well-being. Practicing mindfulness, empathy, and patience when our little one is having a bad day and using this as a comforting, nurturing, and teaching moment is an excellent way to teach them emotional regulation through modeling and implementing our healthy emotional regulation practices. As a parent or primary caretaker, it is important to practice self-care in the form of rest, relaxation, and joyful activities that regulate our minds and emotions so that we can be a better example for our child. This enables us to connect better with them, have greater patience during teaching moments, encourage and praise healthy expressions, and improve their self-regulation and growth.

Common Misconceptions on Emotional Regulation

There are many misconceptions when it comes to emotional regulation and expression. Contrary to popular belief, intense emotions are not scary and they should not be buried. Becoming a resilient person means addressing and working through your emotions through self-reflection. Healthy expression decreases emotional turmoil, vulnerabilities, and distress. Think of healthy emotional expression as the care taken when disinfecting a deep cut, applying ointment, and binding it closed to ensure healing. It is essentially a life skill that promotes healing at the root and protects you from negativity or illnesses. Here are a few common misconceptions you should be aware of:

- **Emotions make you weak**: Not giving in to emotions does not make you a stronger individual. Feeling or expressing your emotions does not make you weak or too sensitive. Expressing yourself is healthy and normal. It is a great way to set healthy boundaries in relationships and to learn emotional regulation. Prolonged emotional control increases vulnerability to volatile emotional outbursts. Harboring strong emotions increases emotional and mental distress that affects your mental, emotional, and eventually physical well-being.

- **How I feel is the truth**: Emotional regulation hinges on self-reflection and the understanding of your emotions and context. The way you feel about a decision or interaction does not necessarily mean that it is the reality or the right decision. Overwhelming feelings and anxious thoughts can inhibit us from making the best decisions for ourselves, hinder us from personal progress, and cloud judgment.

- **Clique-based emotional expression**: You do not have to mold your emotions or feelings to those around you. Your innate expression is pivotal to your beliefs and value system. Inauthentic expressions can lead to self-injury in emotional regulation and inhibit your emotional development.

- **Extreme behavior gets things done**: Assertiveness should not be confused with harsh or domineering attitudes. The latter is not conducive to healthy emotional expression and damages relationships. There is a way to be respectfully assertive without stepping into volatile and impulsive emotional expressions and dysfunctional behavior.

- **Negative feelings are bad**: To feel all emotions and express them is good and beneficial to your emotional health. The tricky part is how you express them. The so-called negative feelings such as anger, jealousy, or frustration can be verbalized in many different ways that help you address inner turmoil.

Emotional regulation is important to understanding ourselves, our social circle and our environment, as well as better understanding our kids. Greater emotional regulation and competence allow us to impart healthy emotional expression and habits to our little ones so that they can build on this foundation. Now that you have the basics down, let's move on to the really fun and important part of parenting. Our little ones can have such huge emotions, and it's up to us to help them manage all that they feel. Learn the best tips and tricks to guide your cute but oh-so-complicated little one between the ages of three and five!

CHAPTER 2

Little Steps for Little Ones (Ages 3-5)

—

THREE LITTLE PIGGIES left their mom's house and went out to discover the world. Each little one was different from the other, and it showed in the way they built their houses. One little piggy liked to laze around and built his house of straw. The second little piggy liked to move around but also laze about, too, and he built a house of sticks. These two piggies loved to have fun and be wild together. The third little piggy was a bit more serious and meticulously built his house of bricks. This house was sturdy and had all the trimmings to withstand environmental changes. One day, a big bad wolf was passing by and wanted to enter the little ones' homes.

Little pig! Little pig! Let me in!

But the three little piggies did not want the wolf to come inside. In retaliation, the big bad wolf huffed and puffed and blew a forceful wind against each of the little pig's houses. The houses made of straw and sticks were not able to hold up and fell to the ground. Only the house made of bricks was able to withstand the wolf's mighty blow.

In this age-old tale, each little piggy is symbolic of the type of kids we have. Some have different temperaments and personalities that are clearly shown in the way they express themselves. The houses built by the little pigs are akin to the emotional toolbox of our little ones. Each of the little pigs' houses demonstrates their personalities, how they think, and how they are developing. Kids may struggle to express themselves in a manner we can understand or tolerate. It doesn't help them when we become frustrated with their behavior and retaliate with fury or hurtful actions. Dear parent or guardian, sometimes we can be the big bad wolf. When we haven't helped our little ones express themselves well or created a safe space to tell us what's wrong, their emotional intelligence and regulation suffer. When this happens, small and big events can blow over their fragile houses and leave them vulnerable. Your kid's emotional houses do not have to become impenetrable, but by understanding your kid, you can nurture their specific emotional house and tools so that they retain the expression inherent to them. If we take some time to understand our little one's emotions and help them understand themselves, their emotional toolbox can be just as strong as the third little piggy's house.

Understanding Basic Emotions in Young Kids

Even as adults, we kick and scream and throw things around, and we've been here for a minute! Imagine how frustrated kids are when they are expressing themselves and trying to bring across a message with everything inside of them. During the ages of three to five, your little one is exploring and discovering new places, things about themselves, and how this makes them feel. This process is particularly jarring, but it is only through this exploration that they can cognitively and emotionally mature. As they play and discover life, they are testing both your and their boundaries. This is beneficial for little ones' self-regulation, behavior, and friendships and prepares them for preschool. At ages three to five, you can expect your kid to:

- start expressing whether they are sad, angry, happy, or excited
- understand how others feel
- begin to share and play well with others
- be openly affectionate
- hide the truth when guilty
- be embarrassed at times
- become more anxious when it comes to unfamiliar territory.

Taking Time to Understand Your Little Piggy

When you let your little ones know that Gramps is coming over, this can get them all riled up, and soon excited screams and tiny energized bodies are running rampant throughout the house. Although this is not a negative reaction, the volume of it all may not be to everyone's disposition. You can help your kid lower their tone without taking away their joy by joining their excitement and showing them a less disruptive way to express themselves. Sometimes your kid may wail and screech when you have to leave them for a while. This is distressing for both parties, and even more so when in a public space. The first step is to fully understand your child's emotions, that the little one is anxious and scared of the abrupt change in his or her world, regardless of the fact that you may only be gone for a few hours. A comforting moment, allowing them to fully express themselves, making realistic concessions, and guiding them helps them feel close to you and goes a long way in working through this obstacle. When you know the reason behind your kid's emotions, you can help them work through it with practical advice and a soothing nature.

The skills you impart to your kids and what they acquire along the way teach them how to better express themselves and become more resilient when faced with similar events. You can help your little one develop according to their personality, learning style, and the way they see the world by adopting the Comfort, Play, or Teach model. A comfort stance is taken to set an example of how best to express emotions. When your kid throws a tantrum and is feeling overwhelmed, find out what it is they need or want by being gentle and supportive (Gaumont, 2020). Comfort includes showing them a better way to express themselves after they have dealt with their emotions. A Teach stance occurs through developing a special bond between the parent or guardian and child and enjoying activities together. This bond facilitates a safe and secure environment for them to ask questions and express their thoughts, likes, and dislikes (Gaumont, 2020). A Play stance is taken by giving your little one small tasks and responsibilities. These activities foster self-confidence, independence, responsibility, and perseverance (Gaumont, 2020). The Comfort, Play, or Teach model guides you in your responses and allows the little one to develop his or her emotional skills.

Fostering understanding and recognition in your little ones when it comes to their emotions allows them to better understand themselves and the world. This foundation sets them up for success and allows them to reach developmental milestones. From the ages of three to five, the little ones are slowly becoming more independent, and their curiosity gains momentum. You may start to notice that they have more of an interest in choosing their daily outfits or trying to dress themselves, their hand and eye coordination improves, and overnight they turn into acrobats or world-class sprinters. They may want to socialize more and hang out with their latest best friend, learn to respect others' feelings, display personal preferences, praise themselves, develop a greater attention span, start talking to themselves, follow simple instructions, learn to count, speak in full sentences, create stories, and begin potty training.

Identifying Your Little One's Emotions

Parenting is no walk in the park. Many times, we have to parent in non-ideal circumstances, such as when we are physically and emotionally wiped out or our hormones are out of sync. When your little one refuses an instruction or is engaging in messy or harmful activities you told them not to do, we react in fiery anger or frustration. Recognizing and addressing our own emotions enables us to teach our kids how to recognize and deal with their emotions. When we know how to regulate our emotions, we can understand what we are feeling, why we feel the way we do, and what the best way is to put forth our bubbling thoughts and feelings. Emotional regulation and intelligence allow us to pick up on non-verbal cues, understand different forms of communication, and become better communicators. The ability to mentalize enables us to see the less obvious and become sensitive to our little one's emotions and needs. Helping your kid identify, label, and verbalize their emotions and feelings is vital to their understanding of emotions and social behavior. Self-regulation and managing their emotions well develop a greater attention span, improve understanding of interactions and social cues, decrease emotional impulsivity, increase self-awareness and mindfulness, and allow them to become effective communicators.

When your little one is having a bad day and displays big emotions, instead of simply reprimanding or punishing, let's analyze their behavior. Do they know what it is they are feeling? Do they know the cause of their emotions? As the primary caretaker, are you able to identify the feelings and source of distress in the child? This is the perfect moment to super-parent and introduce an understanding of their emotions! A parent who can mentalize will observe the deeper hurt behind the emotion and behavioral expression and address it. As you nurture and comfort your child, ask them what it is they are feeling. Are they hurt, sad, or upset? What led them to these feelings? Now you can teach them words and synonyms to verbally express what they are feeling and better express themselves to receive targeted comfort and understanding. Let's take a look back at the temper tantrum example in Chapter 1. If your little one was able to recognize their emotions, they would have been able to verbalize if they wanted to cuddle with you, not go to the store because of all the noise, or simply did not like the outfit you picked out for them. Emotional identification tools include labeling the emotion in their behavior, i.e., crying may mean sadness, throwing an object could be anger or displeasure, etc. Making use of emotion flashcards or books on feelings that help them recognize their emotions furthers their understanding.

Talking about your own emotions provides your little one with greater awareness and recognition of their own emotions. Emotional self-reflection and self-awareness guide your little one's behavior when faced with hurt or distress. You can help your little one recognize their emotions by taking note of their nonverbal cues, providing an understanding of their feelings and what they mean, giving these emotions and feeling labels to help self-identification, and listening to your little ones' woes.

Why Recognizing Emotions Is Important

When your kid recognizes how they feel, they are better able to express their distress and needs. The latter is achieved through empathy and understanding from the primary caregiver. When the parent is emotionally responsive, kids can express themselves, release tension, and reduce stressed internal systems. Healthy expression and emotion recognition affect the health of their bodies as well. Greater emotional understanding produces less aggressive behavior and increases empathy and social skills. Understanding emotions guides our little ones in deciphering between right and wrong.

There are many long-term benefits to recognizing emotions and healthy expressions. When your little one can recognize their emotions, they experience a decrease in anxious thoughts and behavior, emotional intelligence improves, they acquire self-soothing techniques, minimize negative behavior, develop good mental and physical health, and set the foundation for long-term healthy habits and a positive outlook on life.

Identifying Emotional Triggers

Triggers can be concepts, environments, people, and thoughts that cause negative feelings and emotional outbursts. Emotional triggers are associated with negative emotions and are in response to sensory stimuli that cause responses such as anger, fury, jealousy, frustration, or hysteria. Triggers relate to emotional reactions that do not feel aligned with what's happening (Cooks-Campbell, 2023). It is often based on your perception of reality and emotional scars. Emotional triggers can be trauma, fear, negative memories or experiences, stressful situations, grief, or a response to change (Cooks-Campbell, 2023). A trigger response can be identified through behaviors such as panic, running away, visible fear, panic attacks, swift mood changes, and emotional outbursts of sadness or anger.

For kids, emotional triggers can be a little different. These triggers are largely in response to physical hurt, feelings of neglect or loneliness, being reprimanded, feeling overwhelmed or overstimulated, a change in their routine, hunger, or not getting their way. These triggers cause emotional outbursts such as crying, screaming, temper tantrums, anger, or ignoring your presence. Witnessing and identifying your little one's triggers can be like moving through a minefield and can just as well have you on edge. Identifying and working through triggers can be done by observing warning signs and patterns before they get all worked up, learning to understand why this is so triggering for your little one and helping them make sense of it all, and talking to them about their feelings. Identifying and understanding emotional triggers can change the way they react to them and manage their emotions.

Practical Tips for Dealing With Triggers

When identifying your kid's triggers, it's important to take an objective stance and implement a plan of action. Kids have different temperaments, interests, and skills, and their triggers differ as well. Here are a few ways to help identify and work through triggers:

- Using your supersleuth abilities, take note of the little patterns that build up to the trigger.
- Jot down patterns you have observed over time.
- Gain access to professional insight.
- Create a plan to guide your little one through the distressing period.
- Use calming techniques and mindful practices.
- Empathize with what is frustrating them.
- Validate your little ones' emotions and feelings.

An awareness of your emotions, understanding them, and implementing healthy behavior and expression are vital to self-development and growth. Besides encouraging emotional regulation and emotional intelligence, understanding emotional triggers enhances mental and emotional health. As your little one develops, this understanding allows his or her social skills and behavior to flourish through the development of healthy and positive habits that benefit them throughout maturity.

Simple Ways for Kids to Express Feelings

By teaching your kid how to express themselves, you are building their mental toolbox of emotions and broadening their scope of feelings. This helps them differentiate between minor or major events and feelings and how best to react to express themselves. When they are not able to express themselves visually or verbally, it can be hard for both parties to understand the point of contention or how to remedy it. Here are a few ways to teach your kid to express themselves well:

- identifying different emotions in themselves
- showing them physical representations of different emotions and feelings
- helping them label their emotions
- role-playing different emotions and the causes thereof
- expressing their pain or feelings through drawings
- teaching them emotion-linked colors
- modeling positive behavior and healthy emotional expression

Emotion teaching moments can occur during an emotional outburst or as a fun learning activity. Paying attention to emotional cues and expressions creates a safe space for them to express themselves and learn. Between the ages of three and five, your little one is more verbal and enjoys story time. Why not encourage learning-based books on emotions and encourage participation before bed? As you go through a few emotions, you can question your little one about instances in which he or she felt like the character in the book. This is a great teaching moment and helps identify emotions in themselves and others. It can teach them healthy emotional expression and positively enforce healthy habits and behaviors (Sword, 2021).

Creating Super-Kids Through Validation

Validating your kid's emotions and feelings allows them to feel seen and heard by you—the apple of *their* eye. In addition to this, praise and affirmations when it comes to accomplishing tasks or expressing healthy behavior foster a sense of trust, connection, and security between parent and child. As their primary caregiver, they look to you for guidance, love, recognition, and approval. Validation provides a space for them to freely express and feel their emotions. You can create a space for acknowledging your little ones' feelings by:

- focusing on them and listening to their monologue
- avoiding interruption, judgment, or interpretation
- restating their feelings to show that you hear them
- refraining from offering opposing commentary, i.e., "But I told you not to do that"
- providing physical trust
- thanking them for telling you (reinforcing the safe space ideology)

When we validate our little ones' big feelings, it shows that we care and take their feelings into account. As a result, there is an understanding that you will listen to them and not minimize or dismiss their sensitive feelings. Invalidating their experiences by ignoring them, bulldozing over their explanations, or not providing comfort deals a crushing blow. Validation is important to create mental, emotional, and physical resilience. Validation of their emotions and feelings contributes to greater mental and emotional health. It strengthens their resolve, boosts their self-esteem and self-confidence, and teaches them to have empathy.

Story Time for Emotional Learning

Story time is often an event your little one looks forward to. Not only do they get to spend quality one-on-one time with you or fall asleep within your comforting scent and embrace, but you ignite their imagination and quench their thirst for adventure. Story time contributes to cognitive and emotional development, improves listening and comprehension skills, fosters social skills, and opens their minds to a whole new world outside of their own. Through story time, your little ones' vocabulary is extended, and they learn and understand complex terms, emotions, and behaviors. This helps develop their reading and writing abilities, providing them with an advantage when it's time for preschool.

Story time allows both parent and child to reflect on the story being told and contrast it to their own reality. This is often an opportunity for the little one to express how the book makes them feel, if they share any similarities to the story, and even make up stories of their own. Introducing routine story time helps develop emotional connections to the story being told and the characters, as well as parents or siblings. It is the best time to develop emotional and social skills through teaching and coaching, as it shapes their minds through interaction. Books that introduce emotional learning and help your little one understand and regulate their emotions have become easily accessible. Check out these eight books that teach emotional learning and help with big feelings for ages two to five—they may even help guide you in coaching your little one through a few hiccups.

1. How Do You Feel - Lizzy Rockwell
2. Llama Llama Mad At Mama - Anna Dewdney
3. My Little Box of Emotions - DK
4. Breathing Makes It Better - Christopher Willard & Wendy O'Leary
5. Big Feelings - Alexandra Penfold
6. Wilma Jean The Worry Machine - Julia Cook
7. How Do Dinosaurs Say I'm Mad? - Jane Yolen
8. Happy Hippo, Angry Duck: A Book of Moods - Sandra Boynton

Teaching Moments in Disguise

The best way to educate your little one on his or her emotions is to do it while having fun and interacting with them. Story time is an interactive session in which little ones can learn new tools and skills, better understand themselves, and develop empathy toward the book characters' plights. Before they reach preschool, you are their primary educator, and through one-on-one time, you are essentially homeschooling them and equipping them with cognitive, social, and emotional skills. It is an opportunity for them to discover and relate to emotional expressions and experiences. It is possible that as you routinely read a book to them and they become familiar with the book, they will pick up qualities and actions within the book. Emotional learning books are essential to such phenomena as they will guide them on how to reflect and behave in different events. Story time provides the opportunity for moral development as you can impart values, belief systems, and healthy habits. Books may engage your little one through questions posed on the pages, but you can also do this by asking your little one about how he or she feels about the character or what he or she thinks will happen before revealing the next page. Using props, changing your voice, or playing with different accents helps your little one retain information better by peaking their attention.

Daily Emotional Learning Through Story Time

You can enlighten your little ones and engage their minds through routine story time. Story time does not only have to be just before bed; it can be through activities throughout the day, personal time with mom or dad, and even trips to the library. Incorporating story time throughout the day can be done by reading a book aloud as motivation while your little one cleans up their playroom. Incidentally, this book is about a princess who loves to dust her bejeweled room so that it sparkles. Making up your own stories is a sure way to have your little one giggling as well as encouraging participation and imagination. You can use or create stories that relate to your little ones' developmental stage, i.e., a book on how to go potty by yourself. Making activities fun builds their understanding and encourages skill development.

Kickstarting Activities for Emotional Control

Kids can understand their emotions, immerse themselves in what they are feeling, acknowledge their emotions, and learn to control their emotions through experiences and activities. Emotional control should not be confused with emotional suppression. The latter does not acknowledge their emotions and limits their emotional competence. Emotional control allows your little ones to learn healthy ways to express themselves emotionally and develop acceptable behavioral responses.

Activities equip our kids with ways to handle difficult emotions, or situations, and setbacks in life. Activities you can implement today to help guide your little one through big feelings are:

- **Mindful walking**: Going outside and getting some fresh air helps release mental and physical tension and frustration felt during big emotions. It is a safe alternative to the little ones throwing toys or hurting themselves and their siblings. Physical exercise and movement stimulate happy hormones that combat negative emotions and feelings. As you are stimulated by the noise of rustling leaves, laughter at the park, or blissful rays of the sun, you are practicing mindfulness that allows you to feel and think about your emotions.

- **Breathing exercises**: When your little one is struggling to catch a breath after being bowled over by big emotions, you can help bring them back down through calming breathing exercises. This can help them center themselves and become in control of their emotions.

- **Talk about their emotions**: After experiencing a big emotion, sit down and discuss what it is they are feeling. This allows them to identify the emotions by themselves. Your vulnerability to your emotions allows them to be vulnerable and learn to control their behavior.

- **Practicing self-care**: Perhaps the first week at daycare made your little one anxious and sad. Self-care practices help revitalize ourselves by prioritizing positive feelings and emotions after experiencing negative ones. Self-care routines teach them that they can change their narrative and exhale negative feelings. Self-care activities to boost positivity may include their favorite activities, i.e., getting an ice cream cone, having a beach day, or a Disney movie night.

- **Create an emotions chart**: An emotions chart displays different emotions. It can be a chart where they place stickers with the correct corresponding emotion block, or it can be a chart in which they can identify their own current emotions after an outburst. The chart helps them identify emotions so that they can better understand their feelings and deal with them.

- **Calming corner**: A calming corner is not a time-out corner or punishment after a temper tantrum. It is a happy place where they can self-reflect on their emotions and behavior. A calming corner does not have to be isolated; it can have a comforting sensory toy, calming colors, and soft pillows. You can sit with them, provide comfort, and talk them through their emotions. This teaches them to deal with their thoughts and emotions before exploding with big emotions.

- **Using sensory bins**: Sensory bins are a calming technique through stimuli. Texture and sound produced from sensory bins release stress and tension through tiny ripple movements. It is similar to self-care routines in that they reduce negative feelings and increase positive ones.

These activities are like coping mechanisms that allow them to function and think clearly through experiencing big emotions. Through this, they can regain a sense of control over themselves and their environment. Make activities a part of your routine to help build your little ones' emotional skill repertoire.

Understanding their emotions and learning to control them can save your little one from a world of hurt. As they mature and enter school, their world becomes more emotionally and socially complex. Help them take on the world by encouraging and investing in their emotional development. Guide them through new emotions and experiences, and boost their self-esteem when conquering school days!

CHAPTER 3

School Days, Emotional Ways (Ages 6-8)

—

T HE FIRST DAY OF SCHOOL is such an emotional day for you and your child. Tears, fears, loneliness, and separation anxiety are experienced on both sides. When your kid enters school, their whole world is flipped upside down. There is a great cultural, environmental, social, and emotional shock that they experience. They are introduced to a variety of stimuli, conversations, and larger-than-life personalities that may have them shrinking into themselves. These early school days can be difficult for your little ones to find their footing, be themselves, and let their delightful personalities shine. Through a healthy emotional and mental foundation, your kid has already built some resilience that allows them to eventually find their way. Believe it or not, by age 5, a child's self-esteem is as well developed as an adult's. Self-esteem is critical to their self-confidence, social skills, and forming social identities. How your child feels in school shapes their lifelong emotional blueprint. In this chapter, you'll discover the tools and tips to help your child build a healthy emotional life.

Decoding Complex Emotions

From ages six and up, your little one can define and verbalize their emotions and feelings. They can verbally express dissatisfaction, anger, and sadness. During an event, they can identify what they are feeling, understand the root of this reaction, and let someone in charge know what happened. They have developed greater self-awareness and awareness of others. This peaks as they are introduced to classes where all sorts of different kids interact and freely express themselves, noticing differences and comparing themselves to other kids who share the same hairstyle, lunchbox, or backpack. Don't be shocked if your little one comes home demanding that you buy a new backpack for them, or they no longer like the Ninja Turtles after seeing that three other kids have the same one! At this age, your little one is discovering how they fit into such a large world.

At this developmental age, your child is becoming more aware of what others do or how they behave and express themselves. At school, they are exposed to many things and may even adopt new habits or expressions. Being exposed to school and so many new people, your kid is learning to adapt their emotional responses and behavior. They become more observant and ingratiate themselves into social circles by regulating their expressions or developing new emotional triggers. Some kids may become overwhelmed at school and shy away from interactions. Others may find that their kids have blossomed with the surrounding vitality and may become less self-involved. New environments mean new emotions and greater emotional adventures for all involved. Strap in, mom and dad!

When you notice these changes in your little one, sit down with them and have a rundown of their day. Let them tell you all about their at-school adventures and new friends, and ask them about their emotions throughout the day. You can help them decode their new or complex feelings through a play-by-play discussion. From asking them how the morning introductions went and how that made them feel to who they sat with during their lunch break, you are helping their self-development by fostering emotional understanding, communicating effectively, and helping build their self-esteem. Encourage them through affection, a listening ear, recognizing their milestones, getting involved with school activities, and supporting them as the next school day looms. Praise for their emotional, social, and physical achievements at school boosts their confidence to succeed on their first solo mission.

Sky Rocketing Social Emotions

With new social interactions, a buzzing environment, and an introduction to many different personalities, your little one begins to develop social emotions. School is filled with newly discovered sounds, smells, and feelings. The shrill school bell, a few kids crying for their mothers, bright colors, a random voice from the metal box above welcoming them to the new school year, and a stranger who is trying to take their parent's place. Frankly, it's a lot to take in, and the novelty takes a while to wear off. Social emotions such as anxiety, frustration, territorial feelings, and jealousy. These are reactions to an unknown environment, people, and kids infringing on your space. If your little one is not used to sharing space or is used to having their own specialized devices or toys, this new environment can be slightly challenging. But don't worry, school is the perfect place to learn greater social emotions such as patience, kindness, generosity, and especially, empathy!

Empathy is a social skill developed and refined during these interactive stages. Your little one becomes more aware of their classmates and how they act or react. They are more sensitive to the ripples of emotions felt at different activities or throughout the day. Developing empathy sensitizes them to others' emotions and guides them on comforting behavior to meet specific needs. You can nurture empathy in your little ones by teaching them about all the different types of people and cultures in the world. Talk to them about their day and bring understanding to their emotions felt at different activities or people. Teach them to practice kindness and mindfulness toward strangers by exposing them to new environments outside their norm or school.

School's Impact on Feelings and Self-Esteem

Schools are the ideal playground to build upon and foster your kid's cognitive, emotional, social, and physical development and growth. The vast experiences and exposures coach them through different circumstances and interactions, guide their thinking, develop meaningful practices, and teach them important life-long skills. The schooling system lays a firm foundation that enables your kid to flourish in all avenues throughout their life. As your kid overcomes complex emotions and feelings, they learn to manage different circumstances and cope with stress. Social skills and healthy interaction are encouraged on school grounds. Through this, they learn how to play with each other, and team spirit or sportsmanship is developed. Self-independence and self-advocacy are cemented through classroom activities or projects and leadership roles. At school, your kid develops an additional family that fosters deeper connections and a sense of belonging (Flook, 2019). As such, they adopt a more positive outlook toward school, new adventures, and a readiness to tackle any obstacle that comes their way.

At every level of schooling, new experiences are waiting for your kid. Classes are shuffled and their friends are moved, social groups form and are solidified, new learning concepts are introduced, homework is increased, and greater expectations are placed on their tiny shoulders. New challenges arise in peer pressure, academic stress, and social anxiety. This can affect their self-esteem and increase their emotional distress. Now and then, their world gets shaken up, but because of a healthy foundation and positive outlook, the ground won't crumble beneath their feet. Feeding your kid's self-esteem will go a long way in helping them manage academic stress and overcome social anxiety.

Tips to Bolster Your Kid's Self-Esteem

Big changes at school can be distressing for kids. When they don't have the best foundation in the form of self-esteem and emotional resilience, their mental and emotional well-being takes a hit and may result in their social skills and academics suffering. Nurturing and bolstering kids' self-esteem and emotional resilience is pivotal to creating superhero kids!

Self-esteem

A healthy dose of self-esteem is essential to your child thriving in school and in life. When kids lack self-esteem, they may shy away from tasks, responsibilities, activities, challenges, new ventures, and growth opportunities. Decreased self-esteem results in increased anxiety, stress, and withdrawn behavior. Eventually, low self-esteem can hinder their mental and emotional well-being, social skills, development, self-confidence, and independence. As parents, our role is to boost their self-esteem and self-confidence by making them feel safe, loved, accepted, and appreciated. Their self-esteem is bolstered as they are showered with positive attention, and they build confidence in their skills and abilities. Trusting that they will do a job well done makes them feel better about their skills and teaches them responsibility and accountability. Praising them for their achievements is the icing on top of the cake for them! Burgeoning self-esteem is nurtured by parental attention, letting kids participate, and showing pride (Lester, 2022). Here are ways that you can nurture your child and help them develop healthy self-esteem and build resilience:

- **Build competence**: It can be hard to start letting your kid do things on their own. Insert flashbacks of your little one asking you for help with every little thing and staring at you with big, round marble eyes filled with pure innocence and trust. With this memory, it can be hard to not baby them and let them go. Letting them toddle and learn to walk without holding your hand is a form of building competence. Certain things they have to learn on their own. Take a step back, encourage them to try things on their own, and let them figure out a puzzle or choose their outfit. Competence is essential to developing independence and self-confidence.

- **Let them try new things**: Self-esteem is encouraged through new skills and knowledge acquisition. As your kids try new things, their minds are nourished, and they develop tools that can help them at school, in relationships, and in their careers. Healthy risks build their confidence and excitement for new challenges. This way, they are not scared by new adventures or change. When trying new things, they experience new emotions and environments that help them adapt their behavior and thinking. Letting them try new things improves self-development.

- **Encourage them to make their own decisions**: When they make their own decisions, you are allowing them to explore their preferences and discover their identity. They develop independence and accountability as they do this. Furthermore, they discover the consequences of certain actions or choices and learn to make different ones when faced with the same question.

- **Give them tasks and responsibilities**: When they have tasks or responsibilities around the house, you create a space for them to show their competence or work until they are competent. This practice teaches them accountability, the skill to complete tasks, self-discipline, and time management. In the long run, this will teach your kid to turn in their homework or assignments on time. Giving them tasks and responsibilities helps them feel like they are part of the unit and that you value them.

- **Sign them up for social activities they are passionate about**: If you observe an interest your kid has in activities, find the nearest place where it is available. Self-esteem and fulfillment in life go hand-in-hand. Social activities boost self-esteem by doing something they enjoy and honing their abilities in this regard, whether it be dance, karate, or swimming. It helps them develop a sense of identity that builds their self-confidence. In addition, they form social skills and bonds at these activities and develop a sense of belonging.

- **Display unconditional love**: Show your kid that you love them regardless of their mistakes or bad attitude. Knowing they always have a safe space with you allows them to speak about events or people that diminish their self-esteem. Increasing their confidence through unconditional love means complimenting them or telling them they are a fantastic kid outside of them doing an activity that warrants your praise. This nurtures their self-worth and esteem, even when they are feeling poorly.

- **Teach them achievable goal-making**: Setting unrealistic goals for ourselves may have our mental and emotional states dipping. It is important that when setting goals, your child is aware of their strengths and capabilities to reach their goals. When they create realistic goals and achieve them, they receive a bolt of positivity and pride in their achievements, which work towards increasing self-esteem and self-confidence.

- **Offer appropriate praise**: Giving praise helps your child develop a positive attitude and perception of themselves. In turn, this increases their self-esteem and makes them feel good about themselves and what they can do. This is essential to mindfulness and self-awareness. Over-praising and under-praising can be detrimental to your kids' well-being. The former can result in poor mental and emotional health, poor self-confidence, and unhealthy boundaries or habits. The latter can lead to a false sense of security or confidence in their abilities and skills.

- **Embrace imperfections and differences**: Social media can affect the way your kid sees themselves. It can create a dishonest narrative about body appearance, social expectations, perfectionism, and how the world is. Teach your little ones to love themselves by appreciating their imperfections, differences, quirks, or talents. Improve their self-esteem by helping them stand firm in their identity and letting them know that imperfection is human nature. No two people are the same, and they should celebrate what makes them different.

- **Model confidence**: As long as they live, they will look to you for instruction and guidance. When we display healthy self-esteem, our kids model their self-esteem after us. They learn to talk and act in different situations just as we do. This doesn't mean that you need to be perfect at every turn. It simply means that if you want to encourage healthy self-esteem in your kids, maybe you should improve your own, too.

Emotional Resilience

As parents, you want your child to move through life without the many challenges you experienced, but despite our best efforts, we can't protect them from obstacles (Hurley, 2020). Resilience helps them navigate through life's rough seas and commandeer the ship. Emotional resilience teaches kids that they are in control of how they feel or the aftereffects of tumultuous events. By building resilience, they can adapt to and overcome adversity, traumatic experiences, tragedies, hurt, and stressful environments. It enables them to manage big or negative emotions expertly and, in a way, health for their well-being. Your kid needs to experience life's challenges so that they can learn from them. These experiences build self-confidence and emotional competence, and when a new challenge arises, they can face it head-on.

You can improve your kid's emotional resilience by:

- Guiding them to form relationships with their peers, foster connectivity, and display empathy to form social support that builds resilience.

- Creating structure through daily routines that provide comfort during stressful periods or big changes.

- Using self-care practices to bring peace to rioting emotions and center yourself.

- Nurturing a positive self-perception of themselves, their skills, and their abilities.

- Helping them see the good in different events, and fostering hopefulness and gratitude.

- Reaffirming that they come from tough stock and how they will get through it because of how awesome they are.

- Teaching them to embrace change and obstacles by allowing them to take healthy risks.

- Teaching them problem-solving skills.

- Not solving all their problems for them.

- Letting them learn from their mistakes.

- Modeling adaptability for them.

Peer Pressure and Emotional Responses

The people your kid meets at school become like their second family because of how much time they spend at school or doing school-related activities. Many kids will transition into new spaces with these familiar faces and form deep and lasting relationships. Peer pressure refers to how individuals within a social group may be intimidated into doing activities or behaving in a manner they may be resistant to (Hartney, 2022). Peer pressure has negative connotations as it can influence your child's emotions and behavior. Your child wants to feel connected to this extension of their family and may place importance on fitting in. It is natural for them to look to members of their social circle for socio-cultural behavioral cues and adopt them to feel included and respected. It is common for kids to adopt certain behaviors, styles, attitudes, and ways of thinking to assimilate into different social groups. Especially if these are people with whom they share many classes or extracurricular activities. Kids feel pressure to conform to certain ways to feel accepted and avoid awkward or uncomfortable events. Having groups that they fit into often makes school and social transitions easier for them.

How to Guide Your Kid Through Peer Pressure Woes

As kids experience peer pressure, they are finding themselves in a vulnerable position. They may experience internal conflict, and this can be observed in concerning mood or behavioral changes at home. As parents, it is our job to guide our kids through the period and affirm their identity so that they will not fall prey to dangerous peer pressure. You can help your kid when experiencing peer pressure by:

- Developing their self-esteem and self-confidence.
- Affirming their morals, values, and beliefs.
- Getting to know their social circle.
- Listening without judgment and helping them make the right decisions.
- Teaching them to stand up for themselves.
- Creating a safe space for open communication.

The Significance of Peer Pressure at This Age

Your kid may experience peer pressure from a young age. As they are exposed to different people with their own sets of rules, values, and norms, they will compare themselves against their peers. Entering a new school year is daunting, and to not feel isolated, kids integrate themselves into new social circles and activities, and teachers partner them up with different people. To make things easier and enjoy themselves, kids fall under peer pressure. Between ages six and eight, the advent of peer pressure is significant, as they are at the age where they are adaptable and malleable, trust easily, are more sensitive, and can be molded by peer pressure. We must be vigilant about the peer pressure children face at school and openly communicate with our kids what they can expect and how to act. Ensuring healthy self-esteem, emotional competence, and a strong personal foundation will build your little one's resilience to negative peer pressures.

Understanding Teacher Relationships and Emotional Growth

A teacher becomes your kid's school parent. They create a homeroom with an intimate environment fit with comforts, provide your kid's specific seating area, and include them on a birthday chart to make them feel special. Teachers play a critical role in guiding, instructing, and educating your little one. When feeling troubled or facing difficulty, their teacher is the first point of contact for them. Your kid's teacher is aware of them and can tell when they are experiencing negative emotions or poor mental health. Most days, your kid may be a chatty Cathy, but today, they are subdued. If there are drastic changes in their academic work, the teacher notes this and steps in if there is worrying behavior. Their job is to counsel students as they grow and mature and help them integrate their social, emotional, and intellectual growth (Lanier, 1997).

Tips for Parent-Teacher Communication and Collaboration

When an alarming incident at school occurs with your child, if he or she has been disengaged lately or is underperforming academically, your kids will reach out. Both of you want the best for your child and play pivotal roles in ensuring success inside and outside the school-yard. Open communication and participation are needed on both ends to help your little ones when they are struggling. Here are four ways to collaborate with your kid's teacher to better understand their emotional needs:

1. Speak to the teacher about any behavior you have noticed with your child, i.e., My son seems to be struggling to understand his homework.

2. Communicate your appreciation to the teacher for how your kid's writing skills have improved as a result of the teacher's efforts.

3. Ask open-ended questions so that the teacher can answer from his or her perspective, i.e., How well has Bradley been interacting with his peers?

4. Let the teacher know that you will help your kid on your end, i.e., helping them read at night if they are struggling at school.

The Importance of a Strong Student-Teacher Relationship

When it comes to school-related woes, your kid may choose to speak to their teacher, who is on-site and may understand the workings of the school-social system better. If there is a school concert coming up and your kid wants to take part but is having self-doubts about their abilities and is comparing themselves to the others, they may speak to their teacher about their inner conflict and ask for guidance. Teacher relationships are important to student success, as they may see them as a comforting presence. The teacher will guide them through their emotions and boost their confidence. A strong student-teacher relationship encourages kids' social-emotional skills, improves their academic success, makes them look forward to classes, pushes them to excel out of respect for their teacher, guides them through academic stressors, and comforts them when they feel burdened.

Practical and Fun Tools for Emotional Management

A school environment and all that comes with it develops complex emotions that may have your little one feeling out of sorts. To help your little one build resilience and manage emotional turmoil and inner conflict at ages six to eight, you can incorporate breathing techniques, emotion journals, and positive affirmations. Applying these tools will help them in manage their emotions.

Breathing Techniques

Breathing techniques calm down their nervous systems by releasing physical and emotional tension and teaching them emotional regulation by centering themselves. Creative calming techniques include:

- Blowing out candles that require them to blow out big breaths.
- Blowing bubbles that teach them to inhale deeply and blow (exhale) gently.
- Using deep belly breaths that expand their bellies until they resemble a balloon and exhaling in a soft whoosh.

Emotion Journals

Emotional journals keep track of your little one's feelings and identify their school-related triggers. Expressing themselves verbally helps them release complex emotions, analyze them, and learn to understand them. Emotional journals keep track of their daily interactions and how they feel that day. Get them a journal in their favorite color or their favorite cartoon character, get them a cool pen, and encourage them to express themselves on paper through words or drawings.

Manage Positive Affirmations

Boosting your kid's self-esteem and confidence helps them build a more positive mindset and emotional resilience. Positive affirmations affirm self-identity, decrease stress, improve responses to negativity, and overcome emotional challenges. Daily affirmations before school can improve their day and encourage them to participate. Self-affirmations such as "I am smart" or "I can do this" boost their confidence in answering questions in class or taking a leap of faith and signing up for the school play. Incorporate positive affirmations through rhymes and songs at carpool that prepare them to conquer the day!

Every new chapter and developmental age brings new challenges and emotions. At every step of the way, we need to up our game and provide our little ones with tools that allow them to bloom into their best potential. If you thought the Terrible Two's and the school drama were an emotional rollercoaster, you're in for a hoot. In the next chapter, hormones run wild, attitudes reach new levels, and emotions become even more complex! Keep reading for tools and tips to help navigate your kid through these changes and keep a level head. Welcome to the Tweens!

CHAPTER 4

The Tween Scene (Ages 9-12)

—

D ID YOU KNOW THAT the brain undergoes more development during adolescence than at any other stage, except for infancy? The tween stage consists of neurological, hormonal, and physical changes that prepare for adolescence. Adolescence is categorized by the changes experienced between the ages of 12 and 24. Can you remember the great and challenging experiences you went through between these ages? No wonder the tween stage can be such an emotional rollercoaster. This rollercoaster isn't just 'a phase,' it's science. Your kid has to adapt in many new ways and keep up with new emotional, biological, and physical developments. In this chapter, we'll look at how to navigate this critical period.

The Emotional Whirlwind of Tweens

According to neurological research and adolescent behavioral scientists, the limbic system kicks into gear in early adolescence (Backes & Bonnie, 2019). As this part of the brain matures, your child will develop greater self-control, be able to understand the consequences of actions, and better process and interpret complex emotions. But for now, it increases their interest in taking risks and pushing boundaries. Between the ages of 10 and 12, kids experience neurological changes in the limbic system region, which is responsible for increased sensitivity to positive and negative events. The cortical regions of the brain that are responsible for cognitive control and self-regulation develop later on. The decision-making part of the brain, i.e. the prefrontal cortex, which is responsible for making smart decisions, thinking of the consequences, and controlling impulses, has not yet been refined. Therefore, during the tween stage, your child's decisions are greatly influenced by the amygdala, which is associated with big emotions and impulsive and instinctive behavior.

The occurrence of puberty over an extended period causes neuroendocrine changes that result in the maturation of primary and secondary sex characteristics for reproductive maturity (Backes & Bonnie, 2019). Puberty-related hormones influence your preteen's mental and emotional processes and can make them more sensitive to exogenous stressors. These hormones affect adolescents' self-image and how they interact with or are treated by others. How the brain develops during adolescence allows it to become more amenable to the demands and challenges of this developmental stage and increases tweens' vulnerability to risky behavior. Kids learn to control impulses and behavior during these ages by experimenting with risky behavior, which aids their cognitive development. The heightened activity of the hippocampus contributes to a greater capacity for learning and forming habits. Areas of the brain that support planning and decision-making develop in the second decade of their lives. Cognitive control in the form of mature responses, emotional intelligence, and functional memory increases tweens capacity for self-regulation.

Friendships: The Emotional Make or Break

Friendships are important during the adolescent school years. It fosters a sense of belonging, contributes to emotional and cognitive development, and fosters a more positive outlook. Having friendships decreases feelings of isolation or exclusion, lowers the risk of poor mental health, helps your kid foster empathy, and boosts their self-esteem. When experiencing challenging or stressful personal events, teens can help each other find solutions or comfort one another as they navigate adolescence together.

Having healthy friendships is important to resisting peer pressure or adverse risky behavior. Young ones are finding their way through adolescent changes and may be battling with certain impulses. Friends who share these experiences can help them make responsible decisions. Supportive and high-quality social groups create current and long-term positive developmental outcomes and mental health. If your kid is pressured by peers into risky or unhealthy behavior, rampant hormones may encourage these actions, especially if the reward is leveling up in social circles or developing street credit. Ensuring that your kid has healthy friendships helps foster greater emotional intelligence, decision-making skills, self-confidence, and healthy behavior.

How You Can Support Healthy Friendships

Regardless of major attitude changes and perceived independence, kids still need mom and dad's parental guidance and advice (even if they don't want it), especially when it comes to joining the right crowd. As parents, we have an outside perspective and mature understanding of our kid's friendship group and may see certain things our kids do not. Here is how you can support them and help them navigate healthy friendships while remaining unobtrusive:

- Be aware of your child's different social skills, i.e., whether they are extroverted or introverted, timid, lack boundaries, or have attention-deficit/hyperactivity disorder (ADHD), and encourage them to socialize appropriately and in ways best for them.

- Host friendship gatherings at your house or be their designated driver.

- Teach them how to communicate well, stand their ground, practice empathy, model kindness, and acquire problem-solving skills that create and benefit healthy friendships.

- Befriend their friend's parents or take part in school-related activities such as a school dance chaperone.

- Be aware of your child's plans or locations.

- Know how your child is maturing in comparison to their peers.

- Be observant and openly communicate with your child, but do not hover over or stifle them, as this can lead to adverse behavior.

- When telling them 'no', take time to explain your stance or let them know what's standing in the way of your 'yes'.

- Teach them good qualities to value in friendships.

- Support the way your tween likes to socialize or express themselves in activities.

- Model healthy friendships and behavior in your social group.

The Influence of Friendships in Emotional Development

Friendships contribute to your child's emotional well-being and development, create a sense of belonging, and may help them cope with environmental, emotional, and social stressors. Friendships are vital to creating positive feelings at school, supporting mental health, and encouraging learning. They also develop essential life skills such as honesty, open communication, listening skills, empathy, kindness, and conflict resolution. These life skills are important to many areas of their lives and they mature into healthy teenagers and young adults. Children need friendships to develop socially, emotionally, and cognitively. Friendships can factor into how well (or not) your child is doing academically, mentally, or emotionally. Healthy friendships build security and inner happiness, foster deeper connections, and create healthier mental and emotional responses to life's challenges. They foster better emotional responses and competence that improve your child's understanding of others' emotions, perceptions, and actions.

Parenting Tweens: Shifting Gears

In the tween stage, a period between childhood and the onset of the teenage years, you may notice your child's need for independence. They no longer want to be babied, kissed, or hugged in public, their dress style changes, and they start to place importance on social acceptance and appearance. At this stage, kids are developing primary and secondary sexual characteristics, making them a bit uncomfortable in their new skin. The onset of hormonal acne, weight gain, and pubic hair can make them extra sensitive and increase their vulnerability to bullying or peer pressure. As they become more aware of their adolescent bodies and genders, they become more aware of gender ideals and expectations. In this confusing and tumultuous period, our parenting skills need a software update. During adolescence, your parenting style changes as your kid learns to communicate and develops understanding on a new level. The needs of our kids change, and we need to adapt to these changes with them.

As parents, we need to be aware of all that our child may be exposed to at school, on social media, and as a result of rapid physical and biological changes. We need to remain supportive, have open communication, and be our kid's pillar. Being open about your tween's struggles and challenges you have also experienced allows them to feel less alone. They can learn from your examples and problem-solving and conflict-resolution skills and apply them to their woes. In parent-adolescent relationships, interacting with greater emotional variability toward conflict teaches behavioral flexibility or enhances your child's ability to adapt effectively and reorganize their behavior in response to personal and social challenges they are facing (Branje, 2018). They need to know that regardless of all the changes and pressures, they can still come home and express themselves without experiencing judgment. They still need guidance on how to navigate it all. It is important that the household remains consistent and has a secure emotional base by setting up rules, boundaries, and standards for behavior. This structure ensures that regardless of whatever happens outside, they have developed a strong foundation so that even if they stray or participate in risky behavior, they can always recenter themselves.

How to Adapt Your Approach to Suit Your Child's Growing Emotional Independence

Forging independence is important to your child's development into a healthy, functioning, and self-sufficient individual. Developing independence boosts their self-esteem and self-worth, improves their cognitive responses, and teaches them emotional competence. The change from needing your presence and physical comfort to not wanting that or you knowing their private business can be a shocking turnaround. It's important to not see this as rejection but rather as an opportunity to trade in your super-sleuth hat for a detective's coat. Parenting adolescents can require sly tactics and maneuvers to be there for your child without encroaching into their territory.

Successful adolescent parenting finds the balance between helicopter versus hands-off parenting styles. Freedom to explore different avenues and choices is important to a tween's development, and it is even more important for them to know that they still have a safety net in mom and dad. As they experience emotional, physical, and psychological upheavals, your kid may want to see how far they can go before they push you over the edge and try your emotional maturity in a whole new way. You can help your tween develop their confidence in a healthy and self-assured way by encouraging them to try new things, discussing the pros and cons of a decision, teaching them problem-solving or coping mechanisms to deal with challenges and disappointments, and letting them take the wheel now and then. Here are a few different ways you can encourage your kid's emotional independence:

- Let them pay for items at the counter.
- Allow them to choose school-related activities.
- Involve them in setting a curfew.
- Be clear and consistent in setting expectations.
- Give them specific responsibilities.
- Set aside special time with your kid.
- Use indirect questioning to not be intrusive or overwhelm them.
- Listen to your kid as they explain their choices and refrain from judgment.
- Don't be afraid of having those uncomfortable conversations.
- Watch their favorite tv shows with them.
- Don't overreact.
- Encourage your girls to take part in sports.
- Encourage your boys to be emotionally sensitive.

Setting Healthy Boundaries for Tweens

Creating the appropriate boundaries can be challenging as your child establishes their independence while still being fully tied to you financially. When they push your button a little too far with a snappy attitude and empty threats, it can be hard not to bring the gauntlet down and let them know it's my house and my rules. Let's avoid awakening the Kraken and let them find their way by adhering to the basic guidelines of your family. Here are three ways to set a healthy boundary for your kid while allowing them to build their emotional independence:

1. **State values**: Focus on beliefs, values, and morals innate to healthy behavior, traits needed to be a decent human being, and values innate to the family unit. These are probably notions your kid has grown up with, understands, and probably agrees with. Values can be honesty, kindness, or family time.

2. **Value-based rules**: develop rules that support these values and which your kids can abide by as a result of their understanding and belief structure. If family time and connections are valued, a rule can be that everyone has to be home for Sunday lunch and that they should not make social plans in this timeframe.

3. **Age-appropriate consequences**: These go into effect after rules have been broken and may be influenced by the extent of the rule broken. Consequences should be clear, understood, and consistent with each child. This will teach them discipline, how to make better choices, and how to understand the consequences of actions and broken agreements.

Social Media and Emotional Well-being

Kids are exposed to social media at a younger age and during a period when they can be easily shaped or influenced by society. At school, social media plays a great role in how kids dress and talk. It influences socio-cultural conversations as well as social skills, i.e., social terms or lingos. How adept your kid is at social media and trends can affect their social circle, influence, and acceptance. For young kids who are exploring and developing their identity, social media can have many benefits. This includes bonding with others, learning about different cultures and new experiences, fostering creativity and confidence in expression, teaching independence, and being aware of current affairs. Social media can improve your kid's self-esteem and foster a positive mindset. On the other hand, it can also do the exact opposite.

Social media is a ripe playground for negativity, explicit content, uncensored conversations, and bullying, many of which your kid is too young to understand or be exposed to. Social media is a contributing factor to antisocial behavior (decreased physical interactions), stress, anxiety, self-comparison, and decreased self-esteem. If your kid is unhappy at school, seeing people on social media who are flourishing can increase negative thoughts and behaviors. Additional risky effects of social media can be feelings of inadequacy, loneliness, or seeking validation through an online community. Monitoring your kid's social media use or influence can protect them from online negativity or age-inappropriate influences.

Guidelines for Parents in Monitoring Social Media Usage

Restricting your child's social media use can be damaging to their emotional and social skill development. Monitoring their usage is a better way to ensure that they are absorbing good content and promoting online safety. Here are a few ways to keep an eye on your kid's usage:

- Set ground rules for the type of social media they are allowed to use at their age. i.e., YouTube, Facebook, etc.
- Set up a social media account together.
- Have an open dialogue about their reasons for using social media.
- Engage privacy settings on devices that protect them from age-inappropriate material.

- Create your own social media profile to monitor them on the platform.
- Teach them about social blueprints and how to protect their reputation through mindful posts or comments.
- Model your own healthy social media practices.
- Take note of how long they spend on their devices.
- Encourage outside activities that give them a break from social media.
- Create a curfew for social media or phone use.

Behavioral Contracts Concerning Social Media Usage

A behavioral contract is an agreement made between you and your child. It outlines the expectations you have for your child's behavior surrounding certain events or activities. Specific behavior your child struggles with or that you think needs to be improved is at the core of the contract. If the agreement is broken, there are consequences, and if the expected behavior is displayed, there is often a reward. A behavioral contract teaches your kid discipline, emotional regulation, and healthy habits.

Behavioral contracts can be altered into social media behavioral contracts. When you notice that your child's behavior is being negatively influenced by social media or that they spend too much time on their devices, a contract can decrease risky behavior and social media addictions. Social media contracts can teach them to be mindful of what they post or engage in, who they follow or interact with, how certain posts make them feel, the effects long periods of device use can have on their eyesight, and how it can isolate them from the family. This contract can improve their communication with you, state your expectations of them clearly, motivate them to self-regulate, and hold them accountable for their actions. When designing your behavioral contract, explain to them your reasoning and make it fun by having them add their professional signature or fingerprint using food coloring.

Here are examples of expected behavior rules that create healthy social media practices and usage:

- I will not idolize social media.
- I will mindfully post or comment.
- I will turn off/in my phone before bed.
- I will not use social media during family or homework time.

Navigating the Complexities of Bullying

According to US statistics on bullying, one in every five students between the ages of 12 and 18 experiences bullying at school, and as a result, 160,000 kids miss school out of fear of their bullies (Irwin et al., 2021). Bullying decreases vulnerable kids' mental health, self-esteem, and self-confidence, and leads to poor academic results. Within the statistical range, kids reported name-calling, insults, activity exclusion, and physical trauma. School-ground bullies leave physical signs and create behavioral changes you may be able to pick on. When it comes to social bullying, observing signs can become a bit more complicated. Online bullies are known to be more vicious when it comes to psychological games.

The Many Faces of Bullying

There are different forms of bullying and each can be just as detrimental to your kid's emotional, mental, and physical well-being. These are the main forms of bullying that parents need to be aware of:

- **Physical bullying**: This form of bullying is the result of physical abuse such as shoving, hitting, pinching, or beating. It can also be physical damage to property, i.e., tearing apart your kid's math book.

- **Verbal bullying**: Unlike physical bullying, this is an attack on your kid's mind to weaken their defenses. It can include name-calling, hurtful teasing, insults, slurs, or sexual harassment.

- **Social bullying**: This form of bullying can include excluding your kid from social events and alienating them at school or in social circles.

- **Cyberbullying**: This can be from online bullies or trolls that attack your kid's physical appearance or passions on social media.

How Bullying Affects Tweens: Short-Term and Long-Term Effects

The different forms of bullying can affect the way your kid expresses themselves and what they believe about themselves. Physical abuse can cause them to become extremely introverted, not engage in interactions, or make themselves unnoticeable. Verbal and cyberbullying alter the way they feel about themselves as they begin to believe the lies their bullies tell, i.e., that they are stupid, unwanted, or ugly. Social bullying may cause them to retreat from friendships and relationships and stunt their emotional and social development. The consequences of bullying are significant and may have long-term effects. The act of bullying can cause:

- Decreased self-esteem.

- Poor mental health.

- School absences due to incessant bullying.

- Feeling bitter, vulnerable, and frustrated.

- Difficulty forming or maintaining relationships.

- Trust issues.

- Dangerous behavior, i.e. drug use or self-harm.

- Vulnerability to sickness due to constant stress i.e. anxious tummies can lead to irritable bowel syndrome.

Parental Superpowers That Save Your Kid From Bullies

All of the aforementioned significant and long-term effects of bullying can be remedied or avoided by providing the best parental support you can. As parents, we need to be hypervigilant about drastic or alarming changes in our kids, such as becoming more withdrawn, poor hygiene, little to no appetite, unexplained injuries, and signs of physical altercations. Regardless of what is happening at school or in their social space, knowing they have a safe space with you to be comforted and guided can make all the difference. Here are a few tips to help your child if they are being bullied:

- Listen and reassure them that speaking about their troubles is the best solution.

- Make them aware that being bullied is not their fault.

- Don't encourage them to retaliate through violence.

- Encourage activities that improve their self-esteem and confidence.

- Set up a meeting with the teachers, principal, and the parent of the bully.

These guidelines can ensure a healthy and positive trajectory for kids who are bullied. To ensure that it is not your kid who bullies others, it is important to be observant of signs that depict bullying behavior, such as:

- Have far too many physical or verbal altercations.

- Display increased aggression.

- May have a designated seat at the principal's office.

- Acquire new devices or items not belonging to them.

- Lack of accountability or responsibility for their actions.

Preparing for Teenage Years

Adolescence brings on social and emotional changes that affect your child in so many ways. They begin to form their identity through internal and external influences and validation, take on more responsibility, and increase risk-taking behavior. As hormones fluctuate, so do tempers and sensitivities. They learn to read different emotions and behaviors through trial and error in social interactions. The onset of puberty exposes your kid to self-doubt, uncertainty, mood swings, and self-consciousness, and opens their eyes to romantic feelings. The teenage years are a complex and tumultuous period with hair-pulling-inducing attitudes and tearful moments.

Emotional Regulation and the Teenage Years

While hormones affect mood and self-image, social interactions and wanting independence may increase stress and anxiety. This combination of emotions and feelings can be overwhelming for your adolescent. Emotional regulation is essential to understanding and managing emotions, learning empathy, and improving social skills. Emotional resilience allows them to not be drowned by tempestuous emotions and social experiences but instead successfully tackle stressful events.

How Parents and Tweens Can Emotionally Prepare for Adolescence

Even though we have gone through the teenage phase, environments and social climates have differed from your time and have created new complex experiences for your kid. As parents, we need to be aware of what to expect to better prepare our kids for the outside world. Rampant emotions can increase their sensitivity to puberty changes, peer pressures, bullying, and social media influences. When your kid is emotionally equipped to navigate adolescence, they will be able to keep their head above water. Here's how to do just that:

- model healthy emotional expression and competence
- model self-care
- reinforce safe and smart behavior
- embrace failure
- teach them healthy coping mechanisms
- teach them independence and responsibility
- enhance problem-solving skills
- boost their confidence and self-esteem
- provide a safe and stable environment at home

Tween years are full of emotional upheavals and surprises (not the good kind). It may have you hiding away from your volcano of a tween as much as they are avoiding talking with you. Although this period may be a little crazy, it's all part of growing up. In the next chapter, we delve into the connection between emotional regulation and ADHD, a condition that affects many families but is often misunderstood.

Make a Difference with Your Review

Unlock the Power of Generosity

"Kindness is a language which the deaf can hear and the blind can see."
- MARK TWAIN

HAVE YOU EVER THOUGHT about the power of a simple act of kindness? It's incredible how a small gesture can brighten someone's day and even change lives. And guess what? Today, you have that chance!

Ever wondered if you could be a hero to someone you've never met?

That's right, a hero! Someone out there is just like you, curious and eager to learn, especially about managing emotions. They're on a journey to understand and guide the feelings of their young ones, just like you were once.

Hopeful Hearts Publishing is passionate about making emotional regulation a skill accessible to every parent, grandparent, caregiver, teacher and more. My mission is clear: to reach and empower as many people as I can. And this is where your superpower comes into play!

You know, most people choose a book based on its cover and what others say about it. So here's my big ask on behalf of a struggling parent you've never met:

Could you leave a review for "Emotional Regulation for Kids"?

Your review, which takes less than a minute to write, doesn't cost a thing but can be a guiding light for someone else. It could help:

- Guide a worried parent to effective methods for nurturing their child's emotional health

- Offer teachers new strategies for creating an empathetic and understanding classroom

- Reassure grandparents with contemporary methods for connecting with their grandchildren emotionally

- Provide caregivers with a valuable resource for practical advice and emotional support tools

- Contribute to building a community focused on improving children's emotional well-being

Ready to spread some kindness? Here's how to leave your review in under 60 seconds:

Scan this QR code to go straight to our review page:

If you're smiling at the thought of helping someone out there, then you're already a part of Hopeful Hearts Publishing – a community of kind, generous souls. I'm thrilled to have you!

I'm excited to assist you in achieving your goals and making your emotional health journey enjoyable and fruitful. The strategies and insights coming up in the next chapters are something you won't want to miss!

A heartfelt thank you for your support and kindness. Now, let's dive back into our adventure of emotional discovery and growth.

- Your biggest fan, HOPEFUL HEARTS PUBLISHING

P.S. - Here's a fun fact: When you share something valuable, your value in someone's life increases. If you think "Emotional Regulation for Kids" could help another parent, grandparent, caregiver, or teacher, why not share this gem with them? Spread the joy!

CHAPTER 5

The ADHD Connection

—

> *"ADHD is not a damaged or defective nervous system; it's a nervous system that works perfectly well with a different set of rules."*
>
> —Dr. William Dodson, M.D.

THERE ARE MANY MISCONCEPTIONS about children with ADHD. They can be perceived as disruptive, unruly, and daydreamers. Brain development and genetics allow children with ADHD to observe and express themselves differently than we do. This does not mean that they are abnormal or unintelligent; it simply means that they may require different tools to work through life. ADHD is an overwhelming disorder for parents and even more so for the child as they struggle with their emotional control. Children with ADHD can achieve much if they have the best care and support provided to them to excel in life. Emotional regulation helps them bring their impulses and wandering minds into focus and feel in control of their internal and external climates.

Unpacking ADHD and Its Emotional Components

ADHD is a neurodevelopmental disorder that can cause inattentiveness, impulsive behavior, poor emotional control, and hyperactivity in your child. This is the most common form of neurodevelopmental disorder affecting childhood and can last well into adulthood. There are three predominant forms of ADHD that your child may display: inattentive type, hyperactive/impulsive type, or a combination of both (Mayo Clinic, 2019).

Inattentive ADHD affects your child's ability to concentrate and can negatively affect their learning processes. They may struggle with following conversations or instructions and organization skills and can be easily distracted.

Hyperactive/impulsive ADHD affects their emotional and behavioral expressions; they may fidget a lot, jump and run around at inappropriate times, and have difficulty waiting their turn.

The third form of ADHD combines the symptoms of inattentive and hyperactive-impulsive ADHD. Essentially, we have a golden retriever pup on our hands. Children with ADHD may struggle with low self-esteem, troubled relationships, and poor academic performance as a result of a low attention span and emotional incompetence (Mayo Clinic, 2019).

Symptoms of ADHD are:

- trouble sitting still, i.e., fidgeting or squirming
- poor attention and daydreaming
- constantly talking and having expressive thoughts
- make careless mistakes
- struggle to resist temptation
- take unnecessary risks
- forgetful memory

The Relationship Between ADHD and Emotional Regulation

In a 2016 study of 61 children with ADHD, researchers suggested there may be a pattern of emotional dysregulation connected to ADHD symptoms (Lovering, 2022). The frontal-limbic circuit of the brain plays a pivotal role in displaying poor control of emotion, motivation, self-regulation, impulsive behavior, and difficulty in self-control. Deficient emotional self-regulation is used to describe impulsive behavior and self-regulation difficulties associated with ADHD that can make it difficult for kids to excel academically and socially. Negative temperaments, irritability, and emotional dysregulation in children can predict ADHD in later life. The inability to inhibit inappropriate behavior due to emotional impulsivity and dysregulation affects kids into adulthood, and about 70% of adults with ADHD still have difficulties with emotional regulation (Barkley, 2023; Lovering, 2022).

Signs of emotional dysregulation can be:

- poor resilience
- inability to balance emotions
- hyperfocus on conflict
- persistent negative emotions (Lovering, 2022)

Common Myths Surrounding ADHD and Emotional Regulation

As a result of emerging research, we are better able to understand ADHD and all its complexities. In the past, many individuals treated children with ADHD unfairly, as if they acted a certain way on purpose or were being disobedient. Kids with ADHD cannot control their emotions and behavior. They simply see and feel the world differently than us and need someone to help guide them on how to reel it in. Here are a few myths and misconceptions about ADHD and emotional regulation if your kid is diagnosed or if you think they are showing symptoms (Pugle, 2022):

- Only boys get ADHD: This neurodevelopmental disorder is not judged by gender, only by chemical and genetic makeup. Boys are tested and diagnosed more often for ADHD, and this may be a result of gender constructs and boys' externalized behavior. Boys can be more talkative, rowdy, and interruptive, whereas girls are taught internalized behavior and to 'act like a lady'.

- Hyperactivity symptoms are needed for ADHD diagnosis: There are different forms of ADHD, i.e., inattentive ADHD. Additionally, hyperactivity may not be a result of ADHD.

- ADHD does not mean you're a bad parent: There are no scientifically proven links that parenting style can cause ADHD. It is caused by genetic, developmental, and possibly environmental factors.

- ADHD is a learning disability: It is a brain-associated developmental disorder that can make learning difficult due to impulse control and a wandering imagination.

- ADHD medication is bad: Prescribed medication can help your kid focus and pay attention. It gives them a sense of control over their emotions and behavioral expression and allows them to flourish academically, socially, and emotionally.

Emotional Roller Coasters: How ADHD Affects Emotions

Children with ADHD tend to feel their emotions more deeply than others and, therefore, express them in bigger ways. Emotions that make them feel out of control of their bodies can have them crawling out of their skin. Kids with ADHD are aware of their lack of control when it comes to impulsive behavior and are even more aware of what others think about them. This sensitivity may contribute to an increase in emotional dysregulation as they feel the pressure to be 'normal'. But when their brain doesn't function exactly like the other kids, it can be difficult to assimilate their behavior into theirs. Emotional regulation can be a challenge for many developing children, but it is even more so for kids with ADHD. When their teacher announces that it's cupcake day and has brought treats for everyone, some will cheer and clap hands, but someone with impulse control might take it a step further. They might bang on the table, screech in joy, or try to look inside the cupcake container.

When children hit adolescence, rampant hormones and sensitivity to moods may increase ADHD-related symptoms. Thus, it is more difficult to focus in classes or maintain good relationships, as most days they are trying to tamp down *weird behavior*. Emotional control requires superhuman strength to keep a tight rein on your emotions while under academic stress and peer pressure and boost your self-esteem. Adolescence is a critical period for teenagers, and how they act defines their social standing. Not many understand ADHD, and a few blunders on this road can have major effects and affect your kid's social skills and development, mental health, and self-esteem into adulthood.

Strategies for Managing Emotional Highs and Lows

Understanding ADHD and how it affects your child is key to teaching them how to manage emotions and mood swings. When raising kids and investing life skills in them, we must let them experience life and learn how to adapt their thinking, emotions, and behavior along the way. As parents, we cannot protect them from everything, and neither should we. Investing in life skills and tools is even more important for children with ADHD. Being taught these guidelines helps them with their emotional regulation and intelligence. Understanding how to manage your child's ADHD and improve their self-regulation will help them build emotional resilience, boost self-esteem, and promote mental clarity.

The Role of Gratitude, Pride, and Compassion

For kids with ADHD to be self-established and resilient, parents need to sew into their self-worth and self-esteem. They are already aware of just how different they are from the majority of kids at school and how their behavior can be perceived. Incorporating practices of gratitude, pride, and compassion are the first steps to a positive and proactive management of emotional ups and downs. These practices are future prosocial emotions that are important to help your child manage impulsive behavior. Gratitude, pride, and compassion build persistence, cooperation, and empathy in children with ADHD (Buzanko, 2023).

Gratitude

Gratitude is a mindfulness practice that turns our focus away from negative thoughts and emotions and welcomes positivity and well-being into our lives. Children with ADHD are extra sensitive to rejection from others as a result of their differences. Practicing gratitude takes their focus away from the possibility of rejection or exclusion and brings harmony to their nervous system (Buzanko, 2023). When they express gratitude, happy hormones such as dopamine are released, and with continuous stimulation, this can lead to an increase in positivity in how they view the world and themselves. A greater influence of happiness and optimism builds resilience against stress and anxiety.

Gratitude can be practiced by:

- Creating a gratitude jar.
- Identifying five things you are grateful for every day.
- Reciprocating kindness and good deeds.

Pride

Feeling pride in their abilities and achievements helps your kid develop self-control and self-esteem and motivates them to work harder. Praising them and helping them achieve tasks allows them to feel valued and important instead of a burden.

Pride can be practiced by:

- letting your kid master activities they are interested in.
- giving your child important responsibilities.
- telling your kid the different ways they make you proud.

Compassion

Teaching your kid to practice self-compassion is important to understanding their struggles and working through them. This is important for any and every child so they can overcome anxiety and procrastination. Self-compassion allows your kid to build on his or her strengths and imperfections and learn to be patient with missteps.

Compassion can be practiced by:

- modeling team-player behavior (no man left behind!).
- teaching them self-compassion.
- helping them understand their diagnosis.
- teaching them to understand their emotions, behavior, and self-development.

Practical Tips to Help Manage Emotions Better

ADHD causes your child to be frustrated by small things, hyperfocus on them, struggle to calm down, and be super sensitive to criticism or insults (Bhandari, 2023). Raising a kid with ADHD can be overwhelming as you try to equip them with important skills while trying to protect them from insensitive individuals. Knowing how to act, support, and comfort your child through challenging emotions helps your child manage emotions well. Helping them manage their emotions can decrease emotional dysregulation and impulsive behavior and give them a sense of control. Here's how you can help your kid manage their emotions better:

- Learn to understand their behavior.
- Be mindful of their ADHD developmental level and treat them accordingly.
- Provide a stable and consistent home environment.
- Support them through emotional or behavioral challenges.
- Help them identify and label their emotions.
- Be the calm to their stormy expressions.
- Don't downplay their emotions.
- Teach them coping skills, i.e., meditation, deep breathing, journaling, etc.
- If they struggle with a task and have an explosive reaction, let them express themselves and calm down. When they feel in control, they will return to it.

Successful Strategies for Emotional Management

In a Reddit group discussion, parents of children with ADHD discussed how it was to raise their children and implement tools or practices that help them regulate their emotions. A mother of a 14-year-old child found that as his amygdala peaked, aggression increased, and he would often be enraged. She incorporated therapy and cognitive behavioral therapy (CBT) techniques, which helped him manage his emotions. CBT is a form of therapy that helps kids with ADHD understand their emotions. When he decided to use ADHD-prescribed medication, his emotional outbursts and volatility virtually disappeared (Reddit, 2021).

Another user found that it was best to teach her nine-year-old child to recognize his emotions, where they were coming from, and how to constructively handle them. This parent started implementing this practice when he was four. When he comes home with a foul mood, she lets him experience his feelings on his own and does not stifle him but waits for him to come to her when he is ready. When he is ready and has control of his feelings, he expresses himself to her and looks for comfort. She models this behavior by letting him know when she needs a little quiet time to deal with her own emotions so that she doesn't boil over onto other people (Reddit, 2021).

A third Reddit user and ADHD parent is diagnosed with ADHD as well and describes how she implements the same strategies for her child that she does herself. Both often experience meltdowns, and she found it helpful to teach herself and her kid to distance themselves from triggers when they feel their emotional control slipping. This parent can identify their triggers and can help her kid identify their own, understand the emotions evoked, and learn how to pre-emptively avoid big emotional meltdowns. She finds that the best way to help manage both their emotions is to create a safe and comforting environment and let the emotions run their course when you just can't help it. When her kid has a meltdown, she teaches him to have some alone time in his room and sets a five-minute timer where he can work through his emotions. Giving him physical comfort, listening to him express his feelings, and acknowledging his feelings have decreased his frustrations and improved his self-regulation (Reddit, 2021).

Medication and Therapy: When to Consider Them

Emotional regulation tools and techniques go a long way in teaching your kid self-regulation and understanding their emotions and triggers. When your kid is exposed to an overstimulating environment and social pressures and feels overwhelmed by their bubbling emotions, upping your ADHD methods may be the solution. This includes the use of medication and therapy in the form of cognitive behavioral therapy (CBT), which is specially targeted at developing your child's understanding of themselves, promoting mental clarity, and giving them a sense of control.

ADHD-Prescribed Medication

This includes lifestyle changes such as a calming home environment, regular exercise or movement, a balanced diet, sufficient sleep, and most importantly, medication. Specially formulated ADHD medication can improve your child's concentration and emotional impulses and allow them to complete tasks. Deciding to incorporate medication will lift a major weight off your kid's shoulders. There are many ADHD medications available, and finding the right one for your child may require patience and a bit of trial and error, but rest assured that once you do, it can make all the difference (Robinson et al., 2023). ADHD medications made available are stimulants that target the central nervous system, non-stimulants, and antidepressants that target your kid's greatest challenges.

Stimulant Medication

Stimulants help your kid focus their thoughts and distractions and are used to treat moderate-to-severe ADHD. This medication works for up to 80% of people who use it and is especially great for children and teens to excel in tasks, school, and activities (Bhandari, 2023).

Stimulant medications are:

- Methylphenidates such as Ritalin and Concerta.

- A combination of dextroamphetamine and amphetamine, such as Adderall.

- Dextroamphetamines such as Dexedrine, ProCentra, and Zenzedi.

- Lisdexamfetamine such as Vyvanse.

- Amphetamines such as Evekeo, Adzenys, and Dyanavel.

Non-Stimulant Medication

If you find that stimulant medications are not the best fit for your kid or you disagree with the adverse effects, using non-stimulant medication might be your preference. Non-stimulants help your kid with their concentration and impulse control as well (Bhandari, 2023).

Non-stimulant medications are:

- Strattera
- Qelbree
- Intuniv
- Kapvay

Antidepressants

Children with ADHD may be at risk for depression, anxiety, and bipolar disorder. Stressful environments, rollercoaster emotions, impulsivity, and sensitivity to how others regard them increase their stress and anxiety. Antidepressants reduce these negative feelings, and in conjunction with a stimulant, your child can better manage their emotional and mental wellness (Robinson et al., 2023).

The Role of Therapy in Treating ADHD-Related Emotional Upheavals

ADHD-targeted therapy is a way to help your kid develop healthy emotional and behavioral expressions, learn more about their strengths and weaknesses, adopt calming practices and positive thinking, and boost their self-esteem. Working with a specialized therapist helps to build their resilience and self-sufficiency when it comes to managing their emotions. Different types of therapy that will benefit your child's emotional development are psychotherapy, behavioral therapy, and CBT (Lener, 2023).

- **Psychotherapy**: Creates a space where your kid can express their feelings about ADHD, how it affects their interactions, and any problems they have with their peers. Psychotherapy teaches them ways to better handle these relationships and deal with authoritative figures.

- **Behavioral therapy**: This therapy focuses on their responses to certain events and how to behave appropriately and in a way that is healthy to them. These strategies are goal-focused and aim to change negative patterns of thinking and behavior through a rewards-based system. Behavioral therapy teaches suitable behavior through direct feedback and supports positive behavior.

- **CBT**: Focuses on challenges and 'impairments' that hinder them from appropriate or healthy behavior. It guides kids to manage irrational thought patterns that prevent them from focusing and completing tasks, i.e., poor concentration, time management, procrastination, self-criticism, or obsessiveness.

Support Systems and Programs

It takes a village to raise a child, and this village has fancy tools and special programs. For children with ADHD, the best support system they could possibly have is people who care. This lets them feel loved, appreciated, and accepted. Building a support system provides them with individual and practical emotional support. This makes them feel less isolated and 'different', creates a positive influence and mindset, provides healthy distractions, supports emotional regulation, and increases their resilience.

Effective ADHD Support

Being supportive and equipping your kid with skills and healthy behavior can help bring rampant thoughts, emotions, and distractions into focus. This is vital for their learning opportunities and abilities, completing tasks, and self-regulation skills that they will need at every developmental stage. Here are ways parents and schools can provide effective support to kids with ADHD:

- Kids who struggle with hyperactivity can find it difficult to sit still for long periods of time or become extra distracted with virtual learning. Allowing them to move around is a way to avoid triggers, and signing them up for outdoor activities helps them expend their energy.

- Children with ADHD may struggle with social interactions. Providing them with opportunities to freely interact throughout the day can improve their sociability and self-esteem. Extracurricular activities are a great way for them to learn about social interactions.

- When your kid has to share work space with others, it can be distracting, triggering, and stressful. Providing them with their own workstation may improve their focus.

- Monitoring and improving kids' behavior can be done through behavioral classroom management, which uses daily report cards and discourages negative feedback. This is a rewards-based system that motivates kids to behave appropriately.

- Organizational training that teaches them time management, planning skills, and organizing their work improves kids' learning and reduces distractions.

- If your kid struggles to focus on tasks, schools can provide extra time to students with ADHD during tests or examinations.

The Benefits of Individualized Education Programs

Neurodevelopmental and learning disorders can make it challenging for kids to learn, work, and complete tasks at the speed of other kids. If ADHD affects your kid's academic progress, they may qualify for an individualized education program (IEP). An IEP can be created by schools, a teacher, a parent, a child psychologist, or a specialized ADHD educator. IEP is a specialized education service tailored to your child's challenges by setting goals and helping them achieve them to obtain academic success. Accommodations and modifications made by an IEP can be extra writing time, additional reading classes, receiving a different homework project or lower grade math problems, freedom to move around or take a walk when they become hyperactive, receiving extra stationery because they are forgetful, and having individuals grade them according to their developmental stage (Martin, 2023). An IEP essentially provides a great space for them to learn, improve, and grow according to their own capabilities.

Additional Education Support

IEP may be advised when challenges for your kid are too overwhelming or extreme. If your kid is struggling with their attention span and academic work, a 504 section play may be advised if they do not qualify for IEP. Unlike IEP, 504 does not include goals or transitional services that help them in high school, but it does include accommodations related to the classroom, i.e., excludes special education.

These accommodations may be:

- flexible forms of seating, i.e., soft chairs or bean bag chairs.
- a reward program.
- seating students next to a good role model.
- allowing fidget toys or stress balls.
- seating them near the teacher.
- letting them take tests in a quieter space.
- extra time for tasks.
- multiple-choice questions instead of long questions.
- oral exams instead of written exams.

Living and learning with ADHD brings forth complexities and unique challenges for both parent and child. As your kid develops and learns more about ADHD, their emotions, behavior, and self-regulation, they will understand what works for them. There are many tried-and-tested methods applicable to all children for better emotional regulation. Gain a deeper understanding of CBT and DBT in the next chapter.

CHAPTER 6

The Tried-and-True Methods: CBT and DBT

—

C OGNITIVE BEHAVIORAL THERAPY (CBT) is one of the best ways to teach kids about their emotions and how to express themselves. Individual CBT (ICBT) and group CBT (GCBT) treat emotional regulation according to your child's specific needs or challenges. Did you know that CBT has a success rate of 55-60% for treating children with anxiety disorders? (Villabø et al., 2018). For children with anxiety disorders, ICBT and GCBT are the superior methods for combating anxiety and flourishing in their environments. According to the study by Villabø et al. (2018), CBT decreases anxiety over 12 weeks and develops positive results for up to two years. In conjunction with Dialectal Behavior Therapy (DBT), these behavioral therapy treatments will set your kid up for success.

Introduction to CBT and DBT

CBT and DBT are types of talk-based psychotherapy that focus on your kid's mental and emotional processing. These are targeted treatments that help them acknowledge and address unhealthy behavioral expressions and understand the emotions and feelings behind them. These scientifically proven methods decrease the anxiety, frustration, and anger that are behind destructive behavior and thinking patterns. CBT and DBT improve emotional regulation by boosting your kid's self-understanding and acceptance of themselves. By making use of CBT and DBT behavioral tools and skills they can master, your child can improve their self-worth and self-esteem and learn healthier ways to regulate themselves.

Cognitive Behavioral Therapy

CBT is a psychological treatment that targets emotional and behavioral dysregulation. It is often used to treat problems such as depression, anxiety, substance abuse, relationship discord, eating disorders, and mental illness. Additionally, it can be used to treat nonpsychological issues such as irritable bowel syndrome (IBS), chronic pain, insomnia, fatigue, and migraines (Cleveland Clinic, 2022). The concept of CBT is rooted in the interconnectivity of your thoughts, feelings, physical sensations and experiences, and your actions toward negative thoughts and feelings. The latter often keeps individuals in self-destructive patterns and hinders self-development and growth.

Helping your child understand their diagnosis and how it makes them feel and analyzing the self-destructive behavior they may have are the first steps of this therapy (Mayo Clinic Staff, 2019). The therapist works on problematic or challenging areas and sets goals with your child. CBT sessions consist of learning techniques such as coping mechanisms, stress management, relaxation, building resilience, and adopting assertive behavior. It guides your child in working through fears or problems they have interacting with others, and learning to bring calm to their bodies. These sessions last between 30 and 60 minutes, can be weekly or biweekly, and can last up to 20 sessions, depending on your child's needs (NHS, 2022).

Dialectical Behavior Therapy

DBT is a form of psychotherapy that helps individuals who experience intense negative emotions (NHS, 2022). The therapist helps your child understand how their thoughts can affect their emotions and behavior. DBT is used to promote healthy behavior in people with depression, anxiety, eating disorders, substance abuse disorders, and post-traumatic stress disorder (PTSD). This talk therapy is done through group therapy sessions where they are taught behavioral skills, individual therapy where your child's learned behavior is adapted to overcome personal challenges, and phone counseling or coaching in which your child can have a direct line to their therapist and is talked through and motivated while experiencing a difficult situation.

Dialectical behavior therapy teaches your kid mindfulness practices, distress tolerance, and emotional regulation to improve their behavior. This therapy equips your kid with essential skills, practical tools, and thought processes that improve their behavior, such as (Schimelpfening, 2023):

- To accept life as it is and make positive changes. They cannot change the world, but they can change how they react to it or choose what affects them.
- Learn healthy behavioral expressions if they display destructive behavior.
- To focus on changing beliefs and thoughts that are not conducive to their healthy development.
- Accumulate positive and valuable experiences.
- To develop teamwork and communication skills through collaboration in their therapy sessions, i.e., group therapy.
- A valuable skill set that enhances their strengths and capabilities.
- To recognize their positive attributes and strengths, master them, and use them to excel.

The Science Behind CBT and DBT

In most clinical guidelines, CBT is the first psychotherapy largely identified as evidence-based. The results gained from CBT make it the gold standard of its field, and continuous improvements in scientific psychotherapy take key notes from its successful strategies (David et al., 2018). Simply put, CBT is the best form of emotional and behavioral regulation therapy currently in the field. CBT has clear research support and dominates the international guidelines for psychosocial treatments, which makes it the first-line treatment for many emotional and behavioral disorders according to the National Institute for Health and Care Excellence guidelines and the American Psychological Association (David et al., 2018).

The cognitive model of CBT explores the role of thoughts in shaping our emotions and behaviors. It proposes that how we interpret events, situations, and challenges will influence our feelings and behavior. The cognitive model suggests that negative or distorted thought patterns contribute to emotional distress and maladaptive behaviors (Rou, 2023). The behavioral model focuses on the connection between behaviors and environmental factors and how they shape thoughts and emotions, recognizes the consequences of behavior and its impact on mental health, and emphasizes the importance of learning and unlearning behaviors through conditioning and reinforcing practices (Rou, 2023). CBT psychotherapy focuses on present behaviors and emotions using its core principles.

In her Biosocial Theory, the developer of DBT states that invalidating environments can lead to the development of pervasive emotional dysregulation in individuals with a higher biological and emotional vulnerability (Jacobs, 2022). Research in DBT suggests that this form of psychotherapy targets the brain's neuroplasticity and can remap connections between neurons (which are the building blocks of the brain) through therapeutic learning! DBT studies showed that the amygdala (the brain's fear center) had decreased intense reactions to negative emotions as a result of this psycho-therapy (Jacobs, 2022). In people with emotional and behavioral disorders, the amygdala is overactive.

DBT offers personalized therapy by accepting the distress they experience while concurrently selecting healthier ways to express themselves (Jacobs, 2022). It makes use of CBT concepts in under-standing the interactions of emotions, thoughts, and behavior and focuses on improving relationships and acceptance. In examining matters from various angles, DBT teaches techniques for managing feelings, forming connections, dealing with upset, self-acceptance, and awareness that help them transition from contrasting positions (Jacobs, 2022).

CBT Core Principles

The three basic principles of CBT are core beliefs, dysfunctional assumptions, and automatic negative thoughts. Core beliefs may be developed in childhood and are rooted in our self-perceptions, per-ceptions of our environment and our future, and the beliefs we create around these factors. Dysfunctional assumptions are emotional and behavioral cognitive distortions that distort your perception of reality. Automatic negative thoughts are the involuntary and subcon-scious habitual perceptions of your reality (Vogel, 2022).

Achieving the full impact of CBT is done through the application of its ten core principles below (Zayed, 2023):

1. **CBT is based on an individual cognitive conceptual-ization of each patient and an ongoing formulation of patients' problems**: Your child's current thinking patterns and problematic behavior are identified by considering factors such as life experiences and childhood. A conceptualization of your child is formulated based on this information to provide an accurate picture of your child's challenges and is reconcep-tualized at every session as the therapist makes progress and more information is divulged.

2. **CBT needs a strong therapeutic alliance**: A strong bond of trust between the therapist and your child is needed and created for a greater success rate.

3. **CBT places a strong emphasis on participation and cooperation**: Decisions regarding goals and actions are made together. Your child's active participation makes a lasting impact and helps them take back control.

4. **CBT is a problem- and goal-focused therapy**: Specific goals are set during the first session. Goals help evaluate and respond to distorted negative thoughts.

5. **CBT prioritizes present challenges**: The focus is on current problems and challenges that cause distress. Past behavior or experiences are evaluated when dysfunctional behavior or thought patterns are rooted therein or when trying to understand childhood events.

6. **CBT emphasizes relapse prevention, aims to educate the patient to be their own therapist, and is educational**: Understanding the CBT process, how thoughts influence emotions and behavior, how to identify and evaluate their thoughts, and creating an action plan are essential to this therapy.

7. **CBT aims to be time-limited**: When your child's challenges are severe, therapy can range from a few months to years. Typically, anxiety and depression are treated for 6–14 weeks.

8. **CBT sessions follow a set format**: Sessions start with an introduction with mood checks and a weekly brief; the middle of the session consists of reviewing homework, discussing the next set of problems, and creating new homework, and the end of the session elicits feedback of the session and how your child feels going forward. Structured sessions improve the efficiency and efficacy of CBT.

9. **CBT teaches patients how to recognize, assess, and deal with dysfunctional beliefs and thoughts**: Therapists help your child identify key cognitions and adopt rational perspectives through guided discovery by questioning their thoughts to evaluate their thinking.

10. **CBT employs a variety of techniques**: The types of techniques selected by the therapist are influenced by the conceptualization, current challenges, and objectives of the session.

DBT Core Principles

DBT has a set of principles that are the pillars of this type of therapy. These principles are all about centering your child and their emotions, teaching acceptance, helping them identify disruptive behavior and change their thought processes, and equipping them with self-confidence-boosting skills.

The core principles of DBT are (Clark, 2023):

- **Biosocial theory**: This theory teaches that emotional dysregulation is a result of invalidating environments. These environments are ones that put you down, decrease your self-esteem and self-worth, or constantly tell you to get over it, which develops difficulty with expressing emotions and self-regulation.

- **Acceptance and validation**: It teaches your child to be understanding and accepting of themselves and validates their experiences. It teaches them to acknowledge their feelings, create understanding, and teach skills that foster healthy behavior. The therapist will teach your child that they are valuable and accepted just as they are!

- **Behavior change**: If your child exhibits self-destructive behavior, a therapist can identify the behavior that triggers these expressions. Behavior change incorporates behaviorism principles with the intent of modifying destructive behavior and encourages social interactions to learn and assimilate healthy and appropriate behavior.

- **Emotional regulation**: Emotional regulation skills help your child navigate intense feelings and emotions effectively. Learning to identify and label emotions helps them develop better reactions and self-regulation. DBT emotional regulation through mindful practices decreases emotional vulnerability and leads to emotional resilience and healthier behavior.

- **Distress tolerance**: Mental and emotional health challenges can distort your child's perception of reality in the form of cognitive distortions. This can lead to catastrophizing, overgeneralization, a 'should have' mindset (should or should not have done that), and filtering. Distress tolerance teaches soothing techniques that make use of your senses to bring your child back to the present. Distress tolerance can be mindfulness exercises, gratitude, or physical movement.

- **Interpersonal effectiveness**: Interpersonal effectiveness skills teach your kid to communicate better, respect themselves, respect others, and deal with people you may not like. They are taught to be assertive and say 'no', express their needs or feelings, and accept differences of opinion.

Real-Life Examples: Kids Who Benefited

Childhood and school environments can be triggering and trauma-inducing for many kids as a result of their sensitivity or vulnerability to emotional dysregulation. Although the emotional and behavioral expressions may be similar, the emotions, feelings, and roots thereof may differ. CBT and DBT successfully help your child understand their emotions and how to express themselves better for their emotional and mental well-being. Emotional dysregulation, cognitive distortions, and negative behavior can be quite overwhelming for your child and hinder them from flourishing at school and in their friendships, such as in the case of Hannah, but with effective behavioral treatment, she was able to create a more positive outlook on life. Take a look at how CBT and DBT were able to transform these kids' lives and boost their self-esteem! To protect their identities, Amy and Andrew were given pseudonyms.

CBT Successes: "Amy" and "Andrew"

Amy experienced bullying at school, and as a result, this once vibrant and outgoing teen became withdrawn and increasingly anxious. She became afraid of things and no longer wanted to go out or apply for after-school jobs. CBT helped manage her fears by challenging them, evaluating her irrational beliefs, and acknowledging and applying her victories and strengths to manage her emotions and behavior. Eventually, she became confident enough to apply for her first job (Optimist Minds, 2023).

Andrew was a model student at a competitive school, but after a while, the pressure of perfectionism, academic success, competitive peers, and being accepted into a prestigious university got to him. As a result, he developed panic attacks where he would have trouble breathing. For several months, he worked with his therapist and learned CBT techniques that helped him overcome his concerns, reengage with friends, and tackle college applications, enabling him to attend a college out of state (Child and Family, 2020).

DBT Success: Hannah

Growing up, Hannah was always anxious, but at 13, it became overwhelming, and she developed fears of academic failure and started doubting her self-worth. As a result of bubbling emotions, she would lash out or find herself crying often. The smallest things would set her off. Hannah started struggling to sleep and get up in the morning, she neglected her studies because she felt that she would not succeed anyway, and she developed paranoia in her social circle, convinced that no one liked her. Acknowledging that something was wrong and out of her expertise, Hannah's mom enrolled her in DBT sessions. This therapy taught her techniques to manage frustrating or angry behavioral expressions, such as counting down from ten to self-regulate. Managing her emotions helps her to talk about her problems to her mom instead of her previous unhealthy behavior of shouting or screaming. No longer does she let her emotions get the best of her. Thanks to DBT, she has developed a better perspective on the world and is a much more positive, confident, and happier person (Child Mind Institute, 2023).

> I'm a hundred percent a happier person...
> I'm a better student, I'm a better friend, I'm
> a better daughter, sister—everything, really.
> —Hannah

Practical Tips for Parents: Using CBT and DBT at Home

The thought of sending your child to therapy when they are young can be daunting. While professional guidance is ideal as your child is exposed to greater stress throughout childhood and school, there are CBT and DBT tools that you can teach your kid at home (Pietrangelo, 2019; Sunrisertc, 2017). This can tackle self-defeating thoughts, impulsivity, and tantrums with an improved self-image, develop new coping mechanisms and problem-solving skills, and help them gain self-control.

CBT Techniques:

- Use play therapy in the form of crafts and role-playing that engages your child to address problems and create solutions.

- Use trauma-focused CBT that focuses on and addresses behavioral and cognitive issues rooted in trauma.

- Act out desired behavior in distressing events and have your child model your behavior or demonstrate other examples.

- Teach your child to restructure negative thoughts and turn them into positive ones.

- Expose your child to self-identified triggers slowly so that they can learn self-regulation and healthy behavior.

- Breaking up large tasks into small steps.

- Incorporate mindful meditation to help ground your child in the presence of distress and help them recognize positive attributes around them.

DBT Techniques:

- When feeling your kid is overwhelmed and hot as a result of high emotions, use coolness to bring temperature and temper down, i.e., having an ice-cold drink with an umbrella to boost morale or making a splash in the pool.

- Change their body's reaction with intense exercise, which can also be used to release stress and tension, i.e., running it off.

- Use deep breathing practices.

- Incorporate progressive muscle-relaxation exercises.

- Teach them to accept things they cannot change but that they can change their reactions to life's challenges or difficulties.

- Promote a balanced diet.

- Make sure they get enough sleep.

- Teach them that change is constant.

- Develop a solutions-based mindset and teach them that there is more than one way to solve a problem.

- Teach them mindfulness skills.

CBT and DBT Activities to Try Today

Improve your child's self-regulation and encourage self-understanding, self-esteem, and healthy behavior by incorporating the above tools. You can further their emotional and behavioral development by incorporating these CBT and DBT activities with your kid today.

One CBT technique that you can explore immediately is:

- a Recognition Technique of sorting tasks that challenge negative thoughts. This activity helps them write down thoughts and feelings on paper and sort them into a heart bucket or a thought bucket.

- incorporate Connecting Thoughts and Feelings Techniques in the form of a detective game. Describe an event and ask your child to use their super-sleuthing abilities to predict what emotions the character may feel or express (Driscoll, 2023).

A DBT activity you can explore with your kid today is square

breathing. This activity uses your kid's imagination as they picture a square block and breathe to the count of four. Square breathing reduces stress and anxiety, helps them calm down, and feel less overwhelmed (Idaho Youth Ranch, 2020).

In this activity, your kid needs to:

- Inhale for four counts.

- Hold their breath for four counts.

- Exhale for four counts.

- Hold it for four counts.

CBT and DBT methods are powerful in adopting healthier behaviors and cognitive processes that allow your child to be their best positive and self-sufficient selves. These effective tools reach new possibilities when you make them fun and engaging with activities that improve kids understanding and expression of emotions. When activities are fun and engaging, it improves your child's ability to retain information. This next chapter focuses on activities for emotional regulation and just how great they can be for your kid's self-development.

CHAPTER 7

Let's Make It Fun: Activities for All Ages

—

"Play is the work of the child."

—Maria Montessori

T HE MONTESSORI WAY is a form of activity-based education that is powerful for teaching kids about emotions. This approach to play combines learning skills with practical application and having fun (Geneva Montessori, 2022). The role of these activities is not always goal-oriented, but simply to learn and have fun, discover themselves, and learn mindful practices. A combination of play and learning satisfies your child's curiosity while enjoying themselves. Interactive play influences the development of fine motor skills, language development, social skills, self-awareness, emotional well-being, and problem-solving skills, and improves their learning ability. Learning through fun activities can be an enjoyable time for everyone involved!

Fun Games for Emotional Learning

Emotional learning can be made fun with the right motivation, including engaging colors and heart-rate pumping activities. In these activities, your kid is stimulated and ripe for learning and retaining information. Here are 10 games you can try at home and engage the whole family in (Proud To Be Primary, 2022; Kelly, n.d.):

1. **Starfish and tornadoes**: This entails creating a thermometer picture with your child that has a starfish at the bottom and a tornado on top. Each of these objects is indicative of their current emotions and feelings. Ask your child how they are feeling—if they are cool and mellow like a starfish or a tempestuous whirl like a tornado. This helps them identify their emotions and when they are bursting with energy. Now you can brainstorm together about the best way to work off that energy!

2. **Turtle time**: The focus of this game is to act like turtles and slowly observe your surroundings. Alternatively, carry a pair of binoculars, a magnifying glass, or fun glasses to practice mindful observation skills. This improves their understanding of other kids' behaviors and social cues.

3. **The dealmaker**: This activity is a form of compromise that teaches them to understand others' perspectives, compromise, and foster patience and mindfulness. If your kid is demanding to go to the park tomorrow morning but you have a conflicting morning schedule, you can make a deal with your kid! Let them know that unfortunately, tomorrow won't work, but if they wait another day, we can all go to the park and picnic.

4. **Taking turns taking charge**: Let your kids each have one day of the week where they can decide what's for dinner. This helps them develop self-awareness and self-independence and understand others' perspectives, needs, and wants.

Additionally, it teaches them to wait their turn and not poach their siblings' days or display poor behavior when disappointed in meal choices on the other days.

5. **Emotional Jenga:** All you need is a Jenga set and a marker to create this game. On each block, label it with different emotions and feelings. When your child pulls out an emotions block, they can relay what that emotion means and express the events that caused them to feel that way. This helps them identify their emotions and verbalize their challenges, as opposed to bottling them up.

6. **Musical chairs**: This enjoyable game can be turned into an emotional development activity by placing a socio-emotion topic card on a chair. When the music stops, whoever is sitting on the labeled chairs answers the label-related questions. This can teach them a deeper awareness of socio-emotional topics and healthier responses by listening to different perspectives.

7. **Socio-emotional scavenger hunt**: In this version of this fun game, kids spend time searching for acts of kindness! This helps them identify acts of kindness by observing others and checking a list of kind acts. This can be a reward-based game that encourages kind acts in children.

8. **Kindness calendar**: Design a color-coded and sticker-motivating 30-day chart for your child. Each day is a goal for acts of kindness that they need to complete. This can be a 'thank you' day or a day where they bring their grandma some flowers. You can leave a few days blank and they can fill in the kindness act they did on their own for the day. This activity teaches them to be kind to others, especially themselves. It also boosts their self-esteem and self-worth.

9. **Empathy games**: An empathy game can be 'What should I do?' that teaches self-awareness. Show your kid examples of

different events and ask them to use their super-sleuthing skills to identify what matters most in these events and what the best course of action is. This will also teach them choices and consequences as you give them feedback.

10. **Guess the emotion**: This is a sort of 'Who am I?' game that develops cognitive skills and emotional understanding. Create different emotional faces and tape them onto your kids' backs. Not knowing the emotional expression that they are, your kid is tasked with asking others questions to guide them to the right conclusion. This develops their perception of this emotion and how it is understood by others.

Crafts That Express Feelings

Arts and crafts combine kids' active imagination and creativity to create a safe space for emotional regulation learning. Emotion crafts promote the understanding of emotions and feelings through crafts that include facial expressions and the ability to identify and reconcile their own feelings. These crafts help kids understand how emotions are expressed. Here are five emotion crafts you can do within the safety of your home and make use of household items (You Are Mom, 2022).

Clay Faces

Clay or playdough can be used to create different facial expressions and emotions. Teach your child that each clay color can represent a mood, i.e., red can be anger, and yellow can be joy. Create faces with different mouth movements and eyebrow shapes, and incorporate craft tools such as drain pipe cleaners and googly eyes to make this process more fun. When you have completed the different activities, sit down with your child and teach them how to recognize the emotions of these facial expressions. This is a great opportunity to ask when your child has experienced these emotions and how it makes them feel.

For this activity, you will need:

- colored modeling clay
- cardboard to work on
- a wooden skewer for poking eyes
- craft tools you or your kid like (optional)

Spring of Emotions

This is a spring-based flower activity to help your kid learn emotional balance. It involves printing out stencils of flowers, pasting them on colored paper, cutting them out in parts, and writing different emotions on each petal. Talk to your child about the meaning and root of each emotion as they fill in the petals. Place these crafts in their room, calming corner, or on the fridge to help them learn and retain information learned.

For this activity, you will need:

- colored construction paper
- flower stencils
- coloring paper

Drawing and Painting Emotions

Use drawing tools and paint to depict a scene chosen by your child that includes people, friends, or family. As they draw or paint different characters, take note of the different expressions or colors used. Open a conversation about your kid's interpretation of emotions and bring understanding to them.

For this activity, you will need:

- watercolor paints
- drawing pencils
- white paper

Face Masks

Having theatrical, expressive masks around helps your kid identify different emotions. The emotion masks created can be worn or given to your child to act out that emotion. This activity requires you to print out templates of emojis and have your kid color them in. Thereafter, they get their hands dirty by gluing them to cardboard and then attaching the wooden pallet to the back to assemble the faces.

For this activity, you will need:

- printed templates of emotions
- cardboard
- glue
- wooden pallets

Windmills for Managing Emotions

This activity leans toward coping breathing techniques. Blowing on windmills helps them identify their conscious and subconscious feelings by observing how fast or slow the windmill moves because of their breathing. Windmills can be created by drawing a nine-inch square and cutting it out. Mark four diagonals from corner to tip and cut them, leaving a space in the center. Glue the ends of the tip to the center of the square. Cut the thick cardboard into a 1.5-inch wide by 9-inch-long paddle. To bring it all together, make a hole in the center of the windmill flower, insert a brad, and attach the paddle to the back.

For this activity, you will need:

- a black pencil
- a measuring ruler
- scissors
- thick cardboard
- a brad

Outdoor Activities for Emotional Balance

Kids need to learn to recognize their emotions, develop tools to manage big emotions and avoid outbursts or harmful expressions. As their emotional regulation improves, they will learn to be flexible in the face of change, challenges, and distressing events. When a child is faced with sensory overload, their nervous systems cannot regulate themselves, and this often leads to adverse emotional and behavioral reactions. Children who struggle with executive functions, i.e., struggle with planning, organizing, paying attention, and controlling their emotions, are challenged with self-regulation. Outdoor play stimulates children with different sensory inputs, physical activities, and games that teach them emotional regulation skills. Outdoor learning improves their interactions with other kids, develops socio-emotional skills, teaches them patience and empathy, helps them understand failure or loss, and shows them how to follow basic instructions.

Different Outdoor Activities to Benefit Your Kid

At parks and preschools, the playground exposes your kid to new activities to get their blood pumping, feed their excitement, and learn to make new friends. It is a creative and interactive way for them to learn self-development tools and express themselves freely. How many times have you sent your kid to school and they come back with hair in disarray, backpack askew, or multiple mud stains on their clothing? Surely they had the time of their lives with kids their own age and the freedom to feel and work through their emotions before dusting their knees, getting back up, and challenging the Jungle Gym again. Here are a few outdoor activities that teach them emotional balance:

Outdoor Gazebos

Outdoor gazebos are a quiet zone where your child can go and sit, take a breather, and just observe when they feel overstimulated or triggered. It can be a safe space where they go to self-regulate while being protected from the weather (Homan, 2020).

Sensory Spaces

Sensory spaces are places with multiple sensory bins of different materials that teach kids to just be and feel. These materials can be goo, water, sand, beans, or marbles. This sensory exercise practices relaxation and self-regulation through calming and centering your child and encourages self-reflection (Homan, 2020).

Outdoor Social Games

Social interactive games such as tag or hide and go seek teach self-regulation as kids are tested in different emotions throughout these activities. Often, they have to control their temperaments to reach the goal of the game, get themselves to safety, and activate stealth mode. In outdoor social games, children really learn self-regulation skills for problem-solving and coping mechanisms (Your Therapy Source, 2019).

Balloon Volleyball

Replacing a regular volleyball with a balloon in this game allows kids to practice care and patience and exercise impulse control to move the balloon effectively (Rothman, 2021).

Self-Control Games

Self-control games, i.e., Stop and Start games, develop skills such as filtering information, following rules, taking turns, and managing frustrations. These games require kids to listen correctly and respond quickly, managing their loud emotions to become focused. Examples of such games are:

- Simon Says
- Red Light, Green Light

Activities for Special Occasions

During seasonal festivities and special occasions, your kid experiences new events, people, and activities that can overstimulate them or make their emotions start to bubble. Super-parents and guardians to the rescue once more! When your kid starts displaying emotions and behaviors that either make them want to crawl out of their skin or look as if they are about to blast away any minute, this is the time to give them attention and help them address what they are feeling. Here are ways to guide your kid's emotional understanding and development during special occasions (Lewis, 2022):

Scared and Worried Feelings at Halloween

Halloween can be a fun yet undeniably spooky season for little ones. It's all fun and games—finding a costume, painting their faces, and dreaming of endless candy—but every house they visit can be a bit spookier. When they start feeling scared, nervous, or worried, this is an opportune time to walk them through their feelings, encourage them to be brave, and prepare them for the different monsters they could encounter.

Scary feelings can be overcome by creating a supportive stuffed animal who shares the same fears as your child and is used as an educational tool for bravery. Ideally, provide them with a flashlight to light up the darkness, but if it is all too much, give them the comfort they need and slowly introduce them to the spooky season next year.

Appreciative and Grateful Feelings at Thanksgiving

Thanksgiving is a time for gratitude and mindfulness. You can develop your kid's emotional well-being by teaching them what this season means for your family. You can stimulate their thinking by asking them what they are grateful for, how they feel, and what it means to be kind to others. This season can be used to develop empathy, appreciation, and positivity.

Compassionate Feelings During the December Holidays

It can be easy for your child to lose their sense of self when confronted with all the cheer, color, and sparkles of the Christmas season. Even as adults, we don't lose that sense of wonder. This season can be used to teach your child compassion, to be helpful and loving, and to feel connected to others in synchronized happiness. Teaching them about the joys of the season can be aptly done through watching Christmas movies, i.e., The Grinch, and understanding emotions or the value of the Christmas season.

Emotional understanding and self-regulation can be practiced by:

- making a garland or door decorations.
- creating Christmas ornaments.
- writing a letter to Santa.

The role of the parent or guardian is significant in the emotional development of the child. They bring understanding and create a safe space for self-expression. Knowing that you are right there beside them through it all, no matter their fiery explosions, makes all the difference in how they perceive themselves and their abilities. As they get older and are exposed to much more of the world, your continuous support, guidance, and protection are needed. Especially when it comes to the influence of the internet on emotions. Yikes!

CHAPTER 8

Digital Hearts and Minds

—

"One of the greatest benefits of using EdTech in social-emotional learning is enabling students to direct their own learning experiences."

—Andy Larmand

ALL-DAY LEARNING can be such a bore for many kids. They are still at the stage where they want to be active, stimulated, and have fun. In this century, much revolves around technology, and your kid is often invested in the latest gadgets that are making the social circle rounds. Combining their interests with emotional learning can be your secret weapon for navigating your child's well-being and encouraging socio-emotional skills. While the internet can be filled with all sorts of negative influences, education technology keeps your kids engaged with positive learning and equips them with essential life tools.

Digital Emotion: How Tech Influences Feelings

The use of technology on kids can have a range of influences on their cognitive and emotional well-being that can be both positive and negative. Increased use of technology and social media can have adverse effects on your child's development and socio-emotional skills. Internet addiction among young kids is linked to a higher risk of depression, low self-esteem, and loneliness. Additionally, a higher frequency of internet use is associated with reduced physical activity and lower well-being (Children's Bureau, 2019). The internet is a place to connect people and the world, but ironically, it can pull your kid away from reality, develop hyper fixation on internet use, and lead to self-isolation. Self-isolation and a reduction of positive stimuli outside of technology increase the risk of mental and emotional disorders. According to research, one in every five children between the ages of 13 and 18 may develop serious mental illnesses before they reach adulthood. In this group of children (Children's Bureau, 2019):

- 11% are mood disorders
- 10% are behavior or conduct disorders
- 8% are anxiety disorders

Research by Takeuchi et al. (2018) finds that excessive internet use is associated with decreased verbal intelligence and a small increase in brain volume after a few years. This area of the brain is associated with language processing, attention, memory, and executive, emotional, and rewarding functions (Ricci et al., 2023).

A study conducted with 80 British girls aged eight and nine years focused on the effects of appearance-focused games, which resulted in them developing greater dissatisfaction with their appearance compared to girls who were not exposed to such games. This study by Slater et al. (2017) found that appearance-focused games contributed to negative self-image or decreased self-confidence (Ricci et al.,

2023). In a similar study on the effects of internet games, Folkvord et al. (2017) found that advertising games encouraged the consumption of unhealthy foods (Ricci et al., 2023).

Technological influences are not all bad. It creates platforms for children to engage with one another, keep in contact with long-distance family members, and join a community that supports their interests and passions. McNeill et al. (2019) found that limited media viewing of television, games, and apps can be associated with the cognitive and psychosocial development of preschool-age children. Researchers Yu and Park (2017) find that the internet creates a space for kids to exchange ideas and perceptions and adopt different ways of thinking, where they can talk about concerns and increase their social circle. Healthy technology use can be for your child's betterment and improve their cognitive and emotional processing.

Age-Specific Digital Tools

To get the absolute best out of technology that boosts your child's cognitive and emotional development, introducing digital learning tools is the way to go. They enhance your child's language development, improve visual literacy, and increase critical thinking. Innovators have developed new programs and digital apps that educate your child in a fun and engaging way. Here are the different digital tools available for your child and their developmental stage:

Toddlers

These are digital tools for your little ones as they learn to understand their surroundings and what's expected of them in kindergarten (Kawai, 2022; Lascala and Spain, 2023):

- **Elmo Loves 123s:** The 123s can be difficult to learn, but with familiar characters and rhythm, this app will start to tickle your kid's arithmetic brain.

- **Curious World**: This program is ideal for your kid's endless questions and observations. Curious World caters to ages two to seven and provides educational books, games, and activities such as cooking, crafting, and science experiments that assuages their curiosity. This app comes with a parent dashboard that helps you see their progress and achievements.

- **ABCMouse**: This interactive app helps kids between the ages of two and eight learn different topics in math, social studies, art, science, and reading skills. This app has a site progress bar where you can keep an eye on just how well your little one is doing.

- **Starfall**: The main focus of this app is to improve your child's reading ability and understanding of words through printable worksheets. Additionally, this app provides learning in art, language, and math to create a well-rounded kid.

- **Wonderopolis**: True to its name, this app feeds your kids wonder about the world by providing insights and fun facts about culture, nature, and animals, among many other enriching topics. When you subscribe to their email list, you are provided with a 'Wonder of the Day' that fosters your kid's curiosity and Wonder question bank.

- **PBS Kids**: PBS Kids games provides your kids with their favorite and familiar cartoons that teach them all kinds of important skills and information. Popular characters in these games they may recognize are Daniel Tiger and Arthur, which increase their engagement and learning ability.

Young kids

As your kid gets a little bit older, their interests may vary, and they will move to more brain-stimulating and challenging programs. Here are digital tools that meet your kids needs at this developmental stage (Kawai, 2022):

- **Quizzlet**: This is an online learning tool for ages seven and up that creates flashcards, short tests, or spelling quizzes that improve your child's vocabulary and pronunciation. It is an interactive app that prepares them for spelling bees or English tests.

- **Khan Academy**: The Khan Academy learning app for ages two to eight provides interactive activities and videos to improve your child's reading, math, and spelling skills and general knowledge.

- **Funbrain**: This app provides materials based on your child's grade and is an ideal tool for ages six to 14. It provides cute and colorful games, famous and familiar books, videos, and audio for various fun topics. On this app, they can practice skills in early literacy, math, and problem-solving.

- **National Geographic Kids**: If your kid is crazy about world trivia and knowledge, this is the app for them! Nat Geo Kids includes puzzles, quizzes, and action and adventure games that cover various topics such as science, the environment, animals, and science experiments.

- **NASA Kids**: This free website provides games that make learning about science and space fun. This website is ideal for kids who are enraptured by all that is the cosmos.

Pre-teens

When bursting hormones and emotional ups and downs cause tweens to become frustrated, games that distract them from their emotions and develop a healthier mindset can improve their emotional competence. These games awaken their brains, challenge their problem-solving abilities, and teach them positivity.

- **Kahoot!**: This is a game-based learning platform incorporating trivia quizzes and learning games. Additionally, your tween can express their creativity by creating and sharing their kahoots.

- **Lumino City**: Lumino challenges your kid's cognition, attention to detail, and skills through tough puzzles and challenges while keeping them engaged with stunning visuals.

- **Duolingo**: Encourage your kid's language diversity through Duolingo's fun and free language lessons that motivate your kid to complete tasks.

- **HappiMe for Young People**: This app encourages mindful acts and a positive outlook through brain-centered tools and can help them navigate tough situations or feelings as they develop into teens.

Making Emotional Learning Fun: Interactive Tech Activities

Immersive educational games develop social-emotional learning (SEL) within a risk-free environment. Virtual reality provides kids with an instructional approach to learning social-emotional skills and practicing them within the program. Immersive storytelling in games allows them to develop empathy, problem-solving skills, and tools to overcome challenges. When kids engage in virtual reality games that they are passionate about, they can reflect on their own potential and develop a sense of purpose (Froehling, 2023). Immersive activities and virtual reality create experiential learning and a space to learn through trial and error without receiving a punishing backlash. Below are different interactive activities that you and your child can use to make emotional learning fun.

Gamified Apps for Emotion Recognition

Emotion recognition and regulation apps teach your kid how to manage their emotions by teaching emotional skills such as stress management. Digital games improve your child's empathy and increase their prosocial and social skills. In a study conducted with six emotion-balancing apps, On et al. (2019) examined aggression behavior in 72 children of which 35 were clinically diagnosed with disruptive behavior disorders and 37 were typical developing children. The results of this study found that overall aggression was significantly decreased overall and increased levels of enjoyment for both groups (Nicolaidou, 2022).

The following games are beneficial to your child's healthy emotional development:

- **Daniel Tiger's Grr-ific Feelings** uses songs and emotions to foster positive expression, recognition, and understanding of emotions.

- **Zoo Academy** teaches compassion and socio-emotional awareness with the help of cute zoo animals.

- **Mood Meter** encourages kids to reflect on and manage their emotions.

- **Smiling Mind** provides meditation practices that reduce stress and develop social and emotional learning.

Printable Resources for SEL

Enhancing your child's social-emotional learning can be improved with the use of visual aids to better understand their emotions and promote healthier behavioral expressions. Printable resources provide tangible ways to practice and develop their skills.

There are various types of free social skills printables available online. These resources cover different aspects of SEL and cater to individuals of all ages. Let's explore some examples:

- Self-awareness and self-management through emotion and behavior chart resources.

- Social awareness and relationship skills through conversation starters or empathy worksheet resources.

- Responsible decision-making and problem-solving through decision-making worksheets and problem-solving scenario resources.

Easily accessible and well worth your time, printable resources can be found on the following websites and SEL encouraging platforms.

Everyday Speech

Everyday Speech site provides a wide range of free social skills printables that can be used in various settings to encourage daily socio-emotional development.

Common Sense Education

Common Sense Education is a resource center that integrates technology and learning. It is a place where you can find quick activities and lessons from their K–12 Digital Citizenship Curriculum to boost your kid's development.

They cover areas such as:

- Teachers' Essential Guide to SEL.
- Movies to Help You Teach SEL in the Classroom.
- Family Engagement Activities.
- Professional Development Resources.

Teachers Pay Teachers

Teachers Pay Teachers provides content and resources that teach SEL in a digital world. Purchase the Social Emotional Learning Digital & Print Workbook Activities for Google Slides on this site that teach the five core dominants of SEL: self-awareness, self-management, social awareness, relationships, and decision-making in addition to empathy, responsibilities, and self-control.

Extended Notes

Extended Notes is a platform that provides SEL guidance and tools, such as the 5 Digital Tools to Bring SEL into Afterschool. Here are five digital tools that foster social-emotional health in afterschool settings and are available on this platform:

- **Empatico**: This is a free tool to help six- to 11-year-olds build empathy by connecting with others from different cultures and communities through meaningful conversations that spark curiosity, kindness, and empathy.

- **The Social Express**: This program allows kids to interactively work through real-life events to gain foundational skills. It contains 81 webinars to help characters solve social problems and learn important skills such as attentive listening, conflict resolution, and group participation.

- **KidConnect**: This tool teaches emotional and behavioral management, self-regulation, and behavioral modification by teaching kids new strategies to use and self-reflect on their actions, leading to greater emotional self-awareness.

- **Love in a Big World** (LBW): This program offers 24 essential character traits with meaningful activities that support SEL development. LBW empowers social and emotional competency, healthy problem-solving, and making a positive difference in the world.

- **SuperBetter**: This app develops self-growth by turning daily chores and responsibilities into quests and missions. It builds resilience, self-awareness, and self-control by rewarding kids when they achieve goals such as drinking more water or resisting nail biting.

Clever App Store

The Clever App Store is a platform that avails tools needed by schools or districts (or even parents) for digital instructions.

Such tools include:

Everfi: These are standards-aligned games that teach critical 21st-century skills.

Base: This is an evidence-based SEL platform developed by mental health professionals.

Guidance in the Digital Age

To teach your child healthy digital interactions while still fostering emotional growth, use the following strategies:

- Accept and embrace screen time
- Model healthy technology use
- Curate screen time
- Apply parental controls
- Engage your kid in activities
- Create phone-free zones

Staying Updated in a Rapidly Changing Landscape

When it comes to digital advancements and changes, it is important to walk this journey with your child. As parents, we need to make sure that they are exposed to healthy material, that the platforms they are engaged in are safe, and that we monitor how their behavior is influenced by media exposure. This is how you can stay updated:

Stay Informed

A well-informed parent:

- reads up on academic journals.
- follows trusted online platforms, i.e., Science Daily.
- takes note of new behavior and researches it.

Online Communities and Forums

These platforms provide valuable insight and knowledge, allow parents to learn from each other and medical professionals, and allow you to discuss all kinds of child-related challenges.

Join the following well-established and popular online communities that can improve your child's development (Bradshaw, 2022):

Facebook

- Parenting in a Tech World
- Positive Parenting Support and Resources
- Grown and Flown Parents (ages 12 and up)

Instagram

- @BigLittleFeelings
- @RaiseGoodKids
- @Curious.Parenting

Evaluate New Tools and Research

Learning from new research and educating yourself is vital to keeping up with your child and the digital developments that affect them. Many sites spread fear and misinformation, and to make sure that we are guiding our children correctly, we need to make sure that the platforms we engage in are factual, unbiased, and verified. To evaluate new apps or research and make sure the information is credible, we need to:

- ensure that the publisher is well-respected.
- use our own critical reading and thinking skills
- discover if the information is being presented by the original author.
- read from the original author or research paper.

- look at the date of publication and possibly find newer insights.
- research the developers of the app.
- observe the number of downloads or subscriptions.
- read multiple reviews or comments.

Developing a healthy relationship with technology is essential for the way the world is developing. Both of these factors are on a timeless journey of development, so why not do it together? Parental guidance and support as kids learn to navigate the digital era and build resilience make it possible for technology and emotional growth to harmonize. The way you discover and navigate life is a guiding tool for how your child overcomes their own bumps along the road. Follow along to see just how important being your kid's emotional role model is.

CHAPTER 9

Your Role, Your Journey

—

"The best way to make children good is to make them happy."

—Oscar Wilde

A POSITIVE AND HAPPY MINDSET is intertwined with good behavior. If you guide your child in developing kindness, empathy, mindfulness, gratitude, and compassion, they will develop a healthier and more positive outlook on life. Positivity is directly linked to increased happiness. Your child's emotional well-being starts at home. Positive behavior that guides them to a happier life is influenced by parental goodness and model behavior.

Being an Emotional Role Model

From birth, most of their childhood is spent around you. As you cuddle with them, talk to them, and make silly faces, your kid imitates your actions and words. Essentially, you are your child's first teacher. When they are hurt, scared, or excited, who do they call out for? You are their guide and their champion throughout those early years as they begin to understand their bodies and boundaries, and as they get older, they will simply need you more. Being a healthy and positive role model is important to your child's socio-emotional development. Throughout their childhood, the tween stage, and as they become young adults or parents themselves, they will still need your guidance and encouragement. You're their person. Since they were young, they emulated your actions and behavior. The type of role model you are during their pivotal developmental years is important to creating a kid with healthy emotional well-being and resilience.

The way you think and express yourself sets the standard for what your kid will build themselves toward. Are you the best role model you can be for your child right now? If you feel there is room for improvement, here are a few tools that significantly impact your child's socio-emotional skills:

Be kind and considerate: When you offer selfless acts and treat friends and strangers alike with consideration, you are teaching your child to always be kind and considerate of others, have compassion, and learn empathy.

Watch how you speak: Your kid learns how you communicate with and about people in your life. The way you treat these individuals is a blueprint for how they understand how to treat their own friends. The way you communicate with your partner or spouse can influence how they will treat their relationships. And most importantly, the way you speak about yourself, i.e., negative self-talk, can influence how they perceive themselves and can affect their self-esteem.

Walk the Talk: If you are pushing your child toward healthy behavior, managing their emotions, decreasing screen time, or becoming more social, you need to model this same behavior and do activities with your kid that motivate them toward these goals.

Be open about your own past: When your kid is struggling with their emotions, social interactions, or learning struggles, be open about your own similar challenges. If you can relate to them on some level, opening up to them and talking about your own challenges and how you overcame them will boost their confidence and motivate them to get through them.

Have a positive attitude: Maintaining a positive attitude, which they will model, makes it easier for them to develop mental and emotional resilience and problem-solving skills and be successful in their self-development adventures.

Just like our kids, we experience big emotions and triggers daily, but thanks to years of practice, we know where to blow when we're mad, how to treat ourselves to get through it, or use coping mechanisms to bring us back down to one. How we emotionally regulate ourselves or display emotional competence is important to being a good emotional role model. Here are four tips that you can use for effective self-regulation:

- Take time away for yourself—away from your responsibilities or children. These periods are mandatory resets to decompress, maintain thoughts that you are more than just a mother, and enjoy quality time.

- If your child baits you into giving them what they want, don't fall for it! You'll either both be mad real soon or only one will be the victor, and it won't be you. Teaching them that they cannot get what they want through tantrums or manipulation is vital for their socio-emotional development.

- Use breathing techniques to bring mental clarity and self-awareness, and exhale frustrations.

- Enjoy family time through excursions, picnics, or activities around the house, i.e., gardening, painting a room, etc.

- Incorporate movement to boost your physical activity. This can improve mental health and release serotonin and dopamine to improve mood.

Creating an Emotionally Healthy Home

Providing your kid with a home that fosters healthy emotional relationships is just as important as providing them with physical self-development tools. A healthy, happy home is important to their emotional and mental well-being, as this is their primary safe space. A stable, loving home environment teaches emotional regulation instead of control; it allows them to express themselves and learn from gentle rebuke, and it creates a space where they can just be kids. Here are ways to create an emotionally healthy home for your developing kid (Morln, 2020):

- **Provide time, attention, and affection**: Life as parents can get super busy, but we need to still make time to chat and check in with our kids. Devoting a few moments to each child daily lets them know that you care and are present for their challenges and achievements. Low attention and affection often lead to reactive attachment disorder, where you may find them withdrawing from you, no longer coming to you for advice, or becoming hyper independent.

- **Design a space that evokes positive emotions**: A space that evokes positive emotions is clean, well-organized, and exudes peace. This space makes people feel happy and loved, feels homey, and is an encouraging space. An overly cluttered, dingy, or dark environment can increase anxiety, depression, and frustration.

- **Establish clear house rules**: House rules state that certain behaviors are not appreciated or tolerated and help them regulate themselves to avoid breaking the rules. Rewarding their good behavior can motivate kids to steer from negative or unhealthy behavior.

- **Validate everyone's emotions**: Dismissing kids' emotions or silencing their expression can cause psychological harm. Let your kid know that it's okay to feel their emotions. Some of us may have hitters or biters. Validating their emotions means encouraging them to express themselves through healthy behavior without hitting, biting, or hissing.

- **Talk about difficult topics**: Devote time to your kid when they need a shoulder to lean on. Prioritize time with them and create a safe, calm environment where they can open up. Knowing that you are there allows them to discuss social issues, school-related problems, and their mental health. In the future, they will be less hesitant to talk to you as you provide the guidance and support they need.

- **Create predictable routines**: Having a routine and regular schedule decreases their anxiety or frustration around the future or the next step. After a busy day of hard thinking and responsibilities at school, it's great to come home and just be a kid, knowing someone else is there to take care of you.

- **Always go to bed on good terms**: Learning healthy conflict-resolution skills is important to their lifelong development. Teach your kid that conflict is a normal part of family life, that the important part after conflict is relationship reconciliation, and that each person needs to take responsibility for their actions, apologize, and forgive. Settle your kid on the sofa with whoever they are having a spat with and be their mediator. Find out what the root is, guide them in understanding one another, and find a resolution.

- **Have regular happy family meals**: Having regular family time is important for family bonding and communication and should be a place of boisterous interactions. Positive family settings encourage healthy communication and a happier environment. This is the ideal set-up to catch up on everyone's day and talk about new experiences or challenges they face.

- **Say 'I love you' through words and actions**: Constantly reassure your child that they are loved and appreciated in this house. Additionally, you have to show it through special one-on-one time, lots of hugs, and boosting their self-esteem with praise.

Last Tips for the Journey

Raising kids is one amazing journey. Helping them discover themselves and learn self-regulation through trial and error (mostly at our expense) has its ups and downs, but going the distance is truly worth it. Through this journey, not only are they improving themselves, but you are too. Learning to parent and be the best you can be evolves us in many different ways. As they move through their different developmental ages, emotional development continues to take place. It is a lifelong process for everyone, and our socio-emotional skills are refined through every interaction and venture. As your kid goes through different emotional stages, here are a few more tips to improve their emotional well-being (Brookes Blog, 2020):

- **Set small challenges for them**: Provide your child with a few challenges or small changes to their routine. This can improve their self-independence, create trust within themselves, build resilience, and manage their emotions to move forward, complete tasks, and overcome challenges. Examples of small challenges you can set are daring them to run to the top of the hill, challenging them to climb a tree, or encouraging them to wash the dog alone. As they are challenged, your verbal encouragement and praise motivate them to persist and excel until they have reached their goal.

- **Communicate expectations clearly**: Always let your kid know of expectations, rules, or guidelines when embarking on a new task or journey. Reassurance is fostered when they know how to behave or act. An example of this event can be when you are dropping your kid off at a holiday camp. Your rules or expectations can be to always charge their phone, send night-night messages, or call them whenever they feel scared or unsafe.

- **Share appreciation at mealtime**: Meal conversations are personal family times where everyone is relaxed and unwinding. Take this opportunity to share your appreciation of an action you witnessed your child do today, i.e., 'Thank you for helping me tidy the garage today. I couldn't have finished it without you.'

- **Give them a break**: Keeping them busy, challenged, and active is great for their emotional and cognitive development, self-awareness, and self-esteem, but it is just as important for them to have time to be still. Encouraging them to take breaks and have a lazy day encourages them to prioritize their body's needs, i.e., mental and emotional health. Create a fun space, cuddle together, get some treats and popcorn, and watch a movie.

- **Involve children as valued helpers**: Involve your kid in projects or decision-making. This develops their self-confidence and independence and teaches them organizational skills and problem-solving. Additionally, they feel more valued and can adopt orderly thinking. Examples of this can be handing them the grocery list and asking what item is next based on the aisles coming up.

- **Have nighttime check-ins**: After you read them a book, tuck them in, or as you pass their room to turn off their light, check in with your kid about their day, or help them ease their minds about the big day tomorrow. Explore their emotions surrounding daily events and provide them with the space to release frustrating or confusing thoughts so that they do not plague their dreams but improve their ability to find rest.

What's Next? Your Path Forward

The guidelines and themes discussed so far are all about getting to this point—developing children with strong emotional health. This is largely achieved by letting them express themselves, teaching them about emotions, and how best to express themselves in the future. The emphasis on positive emotion is not to say that negative emotions are bad. Experiencing these is pivotal to facing challenges, learning from consequences, and improving emotional health. Finding a balance between positive and negative emotions develops strong emotional regulation. Positive emotions improve our awareness, support our kid's growth, and improve their chance of success. Positive emotions and skills, i.e., compassion, empathy, and kindness, develop greater resilience and ultimately lead to emotional wellness.

Modeling emotional intelligence is important to how your child consumes knowledge as they develop. Home and family are important for nurturing healthy emotional behavior and promoting emotional competence. Don't forget that they have eyes on you all the time and learn their behavior from you. Working on emotional intelligence as a family contributes to strong emotional health. Here are tools to do just that (Lamothe, 2019):

- Notice emotions when they start bubbling, allowing you to label the emotion, handle it, and decide the best plan of action.

- Catch your own self-judgments and turn self-criticism into self-love, compassion, and being kind to yourself.

- Encourage curiosity about thoughts, emotions, and behavior to get to the bottom line.

- Practice emotion regulation coping skills such as meditation or journalism.

- Teach mindfulness activities.

- Strengthen social connections that improve mood and positivity.

- Prioritize rest to improve mood and mental clarity, and reduce emotional reactivity.

As a parent, there are many expectations and responsibilities placed on our shoulders. We want our kids to thrive in a world that may have challenges we are not adept at, and of course, we want them to surpass our own achievements. Ensuring your kid is happy, healthy, and resilient is a tough and important job. When feeling overwhelmed, directionless, or stumped, turning to support groups might be your answer. Parent support groups comfort you with the knowledge that your parental struggles are not an isolated event. On these platforms, you can vent about your challenges and emotions and find understanding in others. You can receive additional tips and tools that work for other parents and see if your child responds well to them. Support groups are non-judgmental platforms where ideas are exchanged and your confidence in your parenting skills is increased.

Parenting is one crazy journey, and you might need all the knowledge and resources available to develop an emotionally resilient, healthy, and happy child in this 21st century. Don't be afraid to ask for help or take the hand of someone reaching out to you. Raising a kid truly takes a village. While this book may be coming to an end, the journey for parents and children is just beginning. Use your parenting guide and enjoy the ride of a lifetime!

Share Your Journey, Empower Others

Now that you have the tools and insights to effectively guide and understand children's emotional journeys, it's time to share your newfound knowledge. Your experience can light the way for other parents, caregivers, teachers, and grandparents seeking guidance in emotional regulation for kids.

By leaving your honest review of "Emotional Regulation for Kids" on Amazon, you're not just sharing an opinion; you're guiding others to a resource that can transform their approach to nurturing emotional intelligence in children. Your review has the power to reach and assist others who are passionate about supporting the emotional development of the young ones in their care.

We deeply appreciate your contribution. The journey of under-standing and teaching emotional regulation is kept vibrant and relevant when we share our knowledge and experiences. And by leaving your review, you're playing a crucial role in helping us to achieve this goal.

Scan this QR code to go straight
to our review page:

CONCLUSION

Raising Champions

TEACHING YOUR CHILD emotional awareness, self-understanding, and healthy behavior at a young age is pivotal for their socio-emotional development. The world can be a scary place for our wide-eyed darlings. As they develop, they become more curious, explore their environments, and push boundaries. Exploring new areas, textures, and objects brings on new experiences and sensations. When these experiences are shocking or frightening, little ones express themselves in the only way they know how at this stage of their development, i.e., screaming like they're dying, rolling on your newly vacuumed rug, flinging their head all the way and turning into a boneless blob, and not answering a single question as to what's wrong. Though these periods can be frustrating and bewildering, it is the perfect time to start labeling their emotions, improving their vocabulary to identify the root of their hurts, and giving them the comfort they need to work through their emotions. Allowing your kids to express themselves is an important step to developing emotional health and self-regulation. This teaches them to acknowledge and address their big emotions and feelings. Only then can they understand and learn positive behavior and communicative skills essential to self-regulation, socio-emotional development, and social integration as they join preschool and burst onto the tween scene.

Nurturing emotional regulation in your developing child is all about instilling healthy emotional habits, teaching them responsibility and independence, and challenging them to improve their cognitive and emotional skills, all while allowing them to still be a kid. Being able to run around, get dirty, let mom or dad take over, and just be is important for their mental and emotional health. Your kid already has many thoughts and confusing experiences as they explore new classes, meet new people, and watch themselves physically change and develop. With many external responsibilities, home is pivotal to your kid's mental and emotional well-being. Health and positivity in these areas are key to emotional regulation and resilience to take on the world.

The world is constantly evolving, and with this come new experiences and challenges. The social expectations and influences your child is exposed to differ so much from what you experienced during your developmental stages. Whether you're in your 20s or mid-40s, the bottom line is that kids need you to be on top of your game. From birth, your kid keeps you on your toes. From midnight cries, diaper explosions, peanut butter mishaps, and streaking to pitch-perfect shrieking, door-slamming, fridge raiding, and days where they just need tons of hugs, parenthood is one wild ride. As they move through various developmental stages, we are right there along with them—waiting with outstretched arms as they stumble through challenges and opportunities for growth. Your child's emotional development is lifelong, as is everybody's. A child's developmental stages are learning opportunities for both them and you. Implementing these guidelines, tools, and tips helps your little one become an emotionally competent child while you improve your parenting skills and style. Raising an emotionally resilient child is the best thing you can do to create an amazing, happy, and strong super kid.

As your little one grows older, the role of the parent becomes increasingly important. At every stage, you can find yourself gathering new resources to aid your child in their development. From finding learning tools and exercises best for your little one's learning style and understanding to teaching them emotion-regulating skills through games, every step of this incredible journey is to make sure your child is prepared—come what may. Use these tools to boost their self-confidence, self-esteem, self-worth, and positive perceptions of themselves, which allow your child to succeed in life—regardless of shortcomings, challenges, or developmental and behavioral hiccups.

You're on the right track! Keep finding ways to sow positivity and healthy habits in your home, and watch how every area of your family's emotional development improves. Make emotional well-being your daily practice. Remember that this guide is not only to improve your kid's childhood experience but also to create well-balanced, independent, and confident adults. Apply this guide to all your kids, share these powerful tips, and let us know how well they are doing in life!

REFERENCES

Backes, E. P., & Bonnie, R. J. (2019, May 16). *The promise of adolescence. Realizing opportunity for all youth.* National Library of Medicine. https://www.ncbi.nlm.nih.gov/books/NBK545476/#:~:text=Adolescence%20%20is%20a%20particularly%20dynamic,the%20neural%20changes%20that%20occur

Bani Salameh, A. K. (2021, February 24). Assessment of temper tantrums behaviour among preschool children in Jordan. *Journal of Pediatric Nursing.* https://www.pediatricnursing.org/article/S0882-5963(21)00049-X/pdf

Barkley, R. (2023, November 6). *DESR: Why deficient emotional self-regulation is central to ADHD (and largely overlooked).* ADDitude. https://www.additudemag.com/desr-adhd-emotional-regulation/

Bhandari, S. (2023, May 15). *ADHD in children: Managing moods and emotions.* Web MD. https://www.webmd.com/add-adhd/childhood-adhd/adhd-children-mood-swings

Bhandari, S. (2023, May 15). *ADHD Medications and Side Effects.* Web MD. https://www.webmd.com/add-adhd/adhd-medication-chart

Bradshaw, P. G. (2022, December 5). *Top 10 parenting groups online.* Troomi. https://troomi.com/top-10-parenting-groups-online/

Branje, S. (2018, January 24). *Development of parent–adolescent relationships: Conflict interactions as a mechanism of change.* Society for Research in Child Development. https://srcd.onlinelibrary.wiley.com/doi/full/10.1111/cdep.12278

Brennan, D. (2022, December 8). *Preschool emotional development.* WebMD. https://www.webmd.com/parenting/preschooler-emotional-development

Buzanko, C. (2023, December 5). *The key to ADHD emotional regulation? Cultivating gratitude, pride & compassion.* ADDitude. https://www.additudemag.com/emotional-regulation-adhd-kids-strategies/

Chassiakos, Y.R., et al. (2016). Children and adolescents and digital media. *American Academy of Pediatrics.* https://publications.aap.org/pediatrics/article/138/5/e20162593/60349/Children-and-Adolescents-and-Digital-Media?autologincheck=redirected

Clark, C. (2023, December 3). *DBT principles—The complete guide*. ASIC Recovery. https://www.asicrecoveryservices.com/post/dbt-principles

Cognitive behavioral therapy (CBT). (2022, August 4). Cleveland Clinic. https://my.clevelandclinic.org/health/treatments/21208-cognitive-behavioral-therapy-cbt

Cooks-Campbell, A. (2023, November 28). *Triggered? Learn what emotional triggers are and how to deal with them*. BetterUp. https://www.betterup.com/blog/triggers

Cours, S. (2023, July 16). *5 Easy social emotional learning activities for kids to do at home*. Better Kids. https://betterkids.education/blog/5-easy-social-emotional-learning-activities-for-kids-to-do-at-home

David, D., et al. (2018). Why cognitive behavioral therapy Is the current gold standard of psychotherapy. *Front Psychiatry*. https://www.ncbi.nlm.nih.gov/pmc/articles/PMC5797481/

Dialectical behavior therapy (DBT). (2019, April 19). NHS. Cleveland Clinic. https://my.clevelandclinic.org/health/treatments/22838-dialectical-behavior-therapy-dbt

Dodson, W. (2023, November 6). *Secrets of your ADHD brain*. ADDitude. https://www.additudemag.com/secrets-of-the-adhd-brain/

Driscoll, L. (2023). *CBT activities for kids: How to explain thoughts and feelings*. Social Emotional Workshop. https://www.socialemotionalworkshop.com/cbt-activities-explain-thoughts-feelings/

Effects of technology on mental health. (2019, September 30). Children's Bureau. https://www.all4kids.org/news/blog/effects-of-technology-on-mental-health/

11 Simple things you can do to support young children's social-emotional skills. (2020, October 27). Brookes Blog. https://blog.brookespublishing.com/11-simple-things-you-can-do-to-support-young-childrens-social-emotional-skills/

First person: How Hannah got happy. (2023, October 13). Child Mind Institute. https://childmind.org/article/how-hannah-got-happy/

5 Crafts to work on emotional intelligence. (2022, May 25). You Are Mom. https://youaremom.com/parenting/raising-a-child/emotionaleducation/crafts-to-work-on-emotional-intelligence/

5 Everyday outdoor activities to practice self regulation skills. (2019, May 16). Your Therapy Source. https://www.yourtherapysource.com/

blog1/2019/05/16/5-everyday-outdoor-activities-to-practice-self-regulation-skills/

Froehling, A. (2023, October 4). *VR for social-emotional learning.* Filament Games. https://www.filamentgames.com/blog/vr-for-social-emotional-learning/

Gaumont, C. (2020, December). *3–4 Years old: Emotional development.* Naitre et Grandir. https://naitreetgrandir.com/en/step/3-5-years/development/3-4-years/child-3-4-years-emotional-development/

Graziano, P. A., et al. (2007). The role of emotion regulation and children's early academic success. *J Sch Psychol.* https://www.ncbi.nlm.nih.gov/pmc/articles/PMC3004175/

Hartney, E. (2022, October 6). *What Is Peer Pressure? Types, examples, and how to deal with peer pressure.* Very Well Mind. https://www.verywellmind.com/what-is-peer-pressure-22246

Haddock, A., et al. (2022). Positive effects of digital technology use by adolescents: A scoping review of the literature. *Int J Environ Res Public Health.* https://www.ncbi.nlm.nih.gov/pmc/articles/PMC9658971/

Homan, E. (2020, January 24). *How the playground can aid children in learning important skills needed for self-regulation.* Pentagon. https://www.pentagonplay.co.uk/news-and-info/outdoor-play-self-regulation

Housman, D.K. (2007). The importance of emotional competence and self-regulation from birth: A case for the evidence-based emotional cognitive social early learning approach. *International Journal of Child Care and Education Policy.* https://ijccep.springeropen.com/articles/10.1186/s40723-017-0038-6

Idaho Youth Ranch. (2020, July 10). *5 DBT skills to help your kids manage stress.* Idaho Youth Ranch. https://www.youthranch.org/blog/5-dbt-skills-to-help-your-kids-manage-stress

Irwin, V. et al. (2021, July 14). Report on indicators of school crime and safety. National Center for Education Statistics. https://nces.ed.gov/fastfacts/display.asp?id=719

Jacobs, S. (2022, November 23). *Science & society: The DBT brain.* Behavioral Psych Studio. https://behavioralpsychstudio.com/science-society-the-dbt-brain/

Kawai. (2022, October 1). *8 Digital tools to help your child to learn.* Turbo Future. https://turbofuture.com/internet/How-Digital-Tools-Can-Help-Children-Learning

Kelly, K. (n.d.). *5 social-emotional learning games to play with your child*. Understood. https://www.understood.org/en/articles/social-emotional-activities-for-children

Klynn, B. (2021, June 22). Emotional regulation: Skills, exercises, and strategies. BetterUp. https://www.betterup.com/blog/emotional-regulation-skills

Lamothe, C. (2019, June 14). *How to build good emotional health*. Healthline. https://www.healthline.com/health/emotional-health#improvement

Lanier, J. K. (1997, July 1). *Redefining the role of the teacher: It's a multifaceted profession. A closer look at what being an educator really means*. Edutopia. https://www.edutopia.org/redefining-role-teacher

Larmand, A. (2023, September 13). *EdTech And social-emotional learning*. Eduporium. https://www.eduporium.com/blog/eduporium-weekly-edtech-and-its-place-in-social-emotional-learning/#:~:text=One%20of%20the%20greatest%20benefits,%2C%20ultimately%2C%20achieve%20greater%20results.

Lascala, M., & Spain, J. (2023, March 17). *18 Fun and educational toddler apps to help kids learn*. Good Housekeeping. https://www.goodhousekeeping.com/life/parenting/g32096855/best-toddler-apps/

Lener, M. S. (2023, March 8). *ADHD treatment options: Therapy, medication, and more*. Healthline. https://www.healthline.com/health/adhd/treatment-overview#1

Lewis, K. (2022, Feb 5). *How to teach kids about their feelings through the holidays*. Speech Blubs. https://speechblubs.com/blog/teaching-feelings-through-the-holidays/

Lovering, N. (2022, May 18). *The connection between emotional regulation and ADHD*. Healthline. https://www.healthline.com/health/adhd/emotional-regul,ation#dysregulation-defined

Martin, L. (2023, September 27). *What to know about an individualized education program (IEP) for ADHD*. Medical News Today. https://www.medicalnewstoday.com/articles/iep-for-adhd#how-does-it-work

Mayo Clinic Staff. (2019, June 25). *Attention-deficit/hyperactivity disorder (ADHD) in children*. Mayo Clinic. https://www.mayoclinic.org/diseases-conditions/adhd/symptoms-causes/syc-20350889

Mayo Clinic Staff (2019, March 16). *Cognitive behavioral therapy*. Mayo Clinic. https://www.mayoclinic.org/tests-procedures/cognitive-behavioral-therapy/about/pac-20384610

Morln, A. (2020, September 2). *10 Ways to create an emotionally healthy home*. Psychology Today. https://www.psychologytoday.com/intl/blog/what-mentally-strong-people-dont-do/202009/10-ways-create-emotionally-healthy-home

Morris, A.S., et al. (2007). The role of the family context in the development of emotion regulation. *Soc Dev 16(2)*, 361–388. https://www.ncbi.nlm.nih.gov/pmc/articles/PMC2743505/

Nicolaidou, I., et al. (2022). A gamified app on emotion recognition and anger management for pre-school children. *International Journal of Child-Computer Interaction*. Elsevier. https://www.sciencedirect.com/science/article/abs/pii/S2212868921001215

Optimist Minds. (2023, January 23). *Five CBT success stories to encourage you*. Optimist Minds. https://optimistminds.com/five-cbt-success-stories/

Overview - Cognitive behavioural therapy (CBT). (2002, November 10). NHS. https://www.nhs.uk/mental-health/talking-therapies-medicine-treatments/talking-therapies-and-counselling/cognitive-behavioural-therapy-cbt/overview/

Parents w/ADHD kids, how do you handle their emotional dysregulation? (2021). Reddit. https://www.reddit.com/r/ADHD/comments/pxx4q6/parents_wadhd_kids_how_do_you_handle_their/

Pietrangelo, A. (2019, December 5). *How Is cognitive behavioral therapy (CBT) different for kids?* Healthline. https://www.healthline.com/health/mental-health/cbt-for-kids#what-it-is

Proud to be Primary. (2022). *16 Social-emotional learning games for kids*. Proud to be Primary. https://proudtobeprimary.com/social-emotional-learning-games/

Pugle, M. (2022, June 6). *8 Myths about ADHD, debunked*. Everyday Health. https://www.everydayhealth.com/adhd/myths-about-adhd-debunked/

Ricci, R., et al. (2023). Impacts of technology on children's health: a systematic review. *Rev Paul Pediatr*. https://www.ncbi.nlm.nih.gov/pmc/articles/PMC9273128/

Robinson, L. et al. (2023, May 10). *ADHD medications for children and adults*. HelpGuide.org. https://www.helpguide.org/articles/add-adhd/medication-for-attention-deficit-disorder-adhd.htm

Rothman, D. (2021, July 29). *7 Outdoor activities for kids to support self-regulation*. Radio Flyer. https://www.radioflyer.com/blog/7-outdoor-activities-kids-support-self-regulation/

Rou, C. (2022, September 13). *Rewiring the mind: The science behind cognitive behavioral therapy.* Quenza. https://quenza.com/blog/knowledge-base/cognitive-behavioral-therapy/

Rutherford, H. J. V., et al. (2015). Emotion regulation in parenthood. *Dev Rev 36*, 1–14. https://www.ncbi.nlm.nih.gov/pmc/articles/PMC4465117/

Schimelpfening, N. (2023, November 2). Dialectical behavior therapy (DBT): Definition, techniques, and benefits. VeryWell Mind. https://www.verywellmind.com/dialectical-behavior-therapy-1067402

Success stories. (2020). Child and Family Counseling Group. https://www.childfamilygroup.com/success-stories

Sunrisertc. (2017, April 24). *Top 5 DBT skills to use at home.* Sunrise. https://sunrisertc.com/top-5-dbt-skills-use-home/

Sword, R. (2021, September 6). *How to encourage children to express feelings & emotions.* High Speed Training. https://www.highspeedtraining.co.uk/hub/how-to-encourage-children-to-express-feelings/

Villab⁻, M. A., et al. (2018). Cognitive-behavioral therapy for youth anxiety: An effectiveness evaluation in community practice. *J Consult Clinic Psychol 86*(9), 751–764. https://www.ncbi.nlm.nih.gov/pmc/articles/PMC6108446/#:~:text=Efficacy%20%20studies%20find%20that%20between,et%20al.%2C%202013).

Vogel, K. (2022, May 6). *The basic principles of cognitive behavioral therapy.* Psych Central. https://psychcentral.com/pro/the-basic-principles-of-cognitive-behavior-therapy

What Is The Montessori Approach to Play? (2022). Mansio Montessori of Geneva. https://genevamontessori.org/what-is-the-montessori-approach-to-play/#:~:text=According%20to%20the%20movement%27s%20founder,integr%20al%20part%20of%20the%20curriculum.

Zayed, A. (2023, July 10). *10 Principles of cognitive behavioral therapy.* The Diamond. https://diamondrehabthailand.com/cognitive-behavioral-therapy-principles/

Made in the USA
Las Vegas, NV
19 November 2024

12156934R00079